VILLAGE ON THE BORDER

Pentrediwaith

Village
on the Border

A SOCIAL STUDY OF RELIGION, POLITICS AND
FOOTBALL IN A NORTH WALES COMMUNITY

by

Ronald Frankenberg

WITH AN INTRODUCTION BY
MAX GLUCKMAN
Professor of Social Anthropology in the University of Manchester

Cohen & West

30 PERCY STREET LONDON W.1

PRINTED IN GREAT BRITAIN BY
BILLING AND SONS LIMITED, GUILDFORD AND LONDON

To

MY FATHER AND MOTHER

Kynn bum kein vaglawc bum hy
am kynwyssit yg kyuyrdy
Powys paradwys Gymry.

Before my back was bent I was bold,
Welcome in beer houses of
the paradise of the Welsh, Powys.

PREFACE

THIS book is based upon research carried out for the Department of Social Anthropology in the University of Manchester. I lived for nearly twelve months in a village in North Wales, for which I have coined the name Pentrediwaith because it will serve to remind the reader of the main characteristics of the village. It is, of course, a Welsh name and means 'village of no work'. I have also changed other place as well as proper names.

All books of this kind owe much to many people besides their author, and I would like to be able to acknowledge them all individually. Some, however, I feel must be singled out for mention. First and foremost of these is Professor M. Gluckman, to whom I owe a great debt of gratitude for his encouragement and guidance in the field and his criticism and help at every stage since. Professor C. D. Forde made many valuable criticisms and suggestions which have been incorporated into the book. Dr. Emrys Peters supervised part of the research and made his knowledge of Wales freely available to me. Anyone writing on Welsh social life must acknowledge a general debt to Mr. Alwyn D. Rees, but I have also the particular debt of his encouragement both before I started and while I was in the village. He has been most generous in sharing his great experience of studies in Wales with a beginner from outside. I am grateful also to Professor W. J. M. Mackenzie and Dr. A. Birch of the Department of Government in the University of Manchester who read the book in manuscript and helped me to avoid errors in their field as well as making many positive suggestions. They cannot, of course, be held responsible for my opinions on such topics or for any errors that remain. Finally, in this category, I would like to express appreciation to all those colleagues especially in Manchester, but also elsewhere, who read and listened to the first draft and discussed and criticized it.

I am especially grateful to the people of Pentrediwaith, who tolerated and even encouraged my curiosity, invited me to their homes and allowed me to participate in their social life. I hope that the book may draw attention to the difficulties of the many villages in North Wales struggling to maintain their existence against economic pressures from outside over which they have little control.

Throughout the study I have had the practical assistance of my wife, who provided a check on my observations and additional material of her own, and acted as a secretary. During the final stages of preparation, I had the secretarial assistance of Miss Elizabeth Corbett of University College, Cardiff, and Miss Carmel Margolis of the Department of Social Anthropology of Manchester.

I am indebted to the University of Wales Press for permission to quote from A. H. Dodd's *The Industrial Revolution in North Wales*; to the Editor of the *Liverpool Daily Post* for allowing me to quote from an article in that newspaper; and to the author and Tavistock Publications Limited for permission to quote from an article by Professor J. A. Barnes in *Human Affairs*.

R. F.

Cardiff,
    March, 1957

CONTENTS

LIST OF DIAGRAMS

INTRODUCTION

THOSE sociologists or anthropologists who, like Dr. Frankenberg, carry out their studies at home, suffer an obvious
disadvantage as against their colleagues who work in Africa or
Oceania. The latter bring to their books a touch of exploratory
exoticism; and even where they tell us something about a
foreign society which, in its general application to humankind,
is obvious, we are interested, and indeed charmed, to learn
that men are the same however strange and bizarre be their
national customs. This advantage is even the lot of those
British anthropologists who write about other European
people, as Dr. J. A. Pitt-Rivers has about a Spanish *pueblo*.[1]
But the student at home is likely to be dealing with facts which
his countrymen know full well, and his conclusions from those
facts may seem equally trite.

Recent studies in Britain do not support this expectation
that we know what goes on in the social life of our country.
Dr. F. Zweig's records of his observations among coalminers
and the people of London[2] were welcomed as 'important and
exciting'. Reviewers have similarly stressed the novelty of the
information produced by a team from the University of Leeds
about a pit-village in Yorkshire[3] and by Mr. W. M. Williams
about a village in Cumberland[4]; and national newspapers, to
the embarrassment of the research workers, have even found
'stories' in some of these reports. We know far less about ourselves in any accurate and detailed way than we like to think.

Dr. Frankenberg's analysis of social life in a North Wales

[1] *The People of the Sierra*, Weidenfeld and Nicolson, 1954.
[2] *Men in the Pits* and *Labour, Life and Poverty*, both Gollancz, 1949.
[3] N. Dennis, F. Henriques and C. Slaughter, *Coal is our Life*, Eyre and
Spottiswoode, 1956.
[4] *Gosforth: The Sociology of an English Village*, Routledge, 1956.

village similarly describes for us a series of situations which we feel we know about; but in fact he makes available, for the first time, detailed information on certain subjects. He studied a village which is important in Welsh tradition, though it is near the English border and its nearest big towns are English. The village is isolated in a valley, but the men mostly go to work in these English towns and no longer work together in local quarrying, milling or farming. He gives us a meticulous account of the attempt of the small Parish Council in this village to deal, during the period of his field research, with two problems which are of critical interest to most British localities: work near home and adequate schooling facilities for the children; though of course these are not technically part of the duties of a parish council. He shows how the discussion of these problems by the councillors and their constituents were affected by religious affiliations and divisions, by class allegiances, and by the place of the local community in the nation as a whole. And he shows how these discussions in the village were affected by relations with the Rural District and County Councils.

When he sought to compare what he had observed with detailed descriptions of the working of other parish councils, or the reactions of people to higher authorities, he found that there were no published accounts of these. I myself have tried to find such descriptions in order to see whether what Colonial Governments in Africa expect of African local councils is in fact done by similar bodies in Britain; and I gather from colleagues interested in this field that, while there are individuals who know how rural district councils and parish councils work, only a series of general statements has been published about them. None of the extant studies of rural areas in the British Isles have dealt adequately with the political life of these communities[1]; and, though Dr. Frankenberg's analysis of

[1] For example, Williams in *Gosforth* describes only 'the indifference to politics . . . clearly related to the remoteness of the parish and its long history as a relatively self-sufficient unit'. Parish councillors in Gosforth appear to be drawn from the upper classes. He lists in a footnote the types of matters dealt with by this council (*op. cit.*, pp. 174 ff. and footnotes). C. M. Arensberg and S. T. Kimball's classic *Family and Community in Ireland* (Harvard University Press, 1940) and *The Irish Countryman* (New York: Peter Smith, 1950) did not deal with politics at all. G. Duncan Mitchell has dealt with parish councils in a rural area in four articles, but he only

Pentrediwaith cannot be applied automatically to any other rural community, it provides a beginning towards a knowledge of what goes on in the political life of villages. This analysis is intrinsically interesting: a dozen comparable analyses would enable us to understand the relation of local government bodies with their constituents themselves.

Here Dr. Frankenberg has been dealing with the attempt of an isolated Welsh village to meet what its inhabitants consider disastrous decisions taken by national and county authorities. These efforts do not exhaust the politics of the village, for the organizing of recreation is of the greatest importance in running the village's life as a community. Hence Dr. Frankenberg relates in detail discussions at committee meetings of the Football Club and the Carnival. Again, no other student of British rural life has published such significant detailed accounts. It is true that we have read about similar situations in novels like Hugh de Selincourt's *The Cricket Match*. The importance of particular recreational activities in symbolizing the unity of villages against other villages is well known, both from these novels and from casual information. Dr. Frankenberg, for the first time, sets out a clear sociological thesis of how the success and failure of these village activities are related to internal disputes and feuds, both between groups and individuals. He found that the villagers ran a series of activities which, though started for recreation, symbolized their desire to be a community: village choir, brass band, dramatic society, football club, carnival. These activities were run in succession, not at the same time. For it seems that each activity in time becomes so bedevilled by the internal group and personal feuds in the village that it can no longer be pursued successfully without leading to an irremediable breach of relationships between some villagers. These may be individuals; they may be groups of kindred; they may be religious groups; they may be the group of village women and the group of village men. Eventually crisis is reached and an activity has to be aban-

---

sketches what happens, and is chiefly concerned to indicate the importance of the problem and to suggest lines of increasing their significance (see especially his 'Social Disintegration in a Rural Community', *Human Relations*, iii, 1950, and also articles in *The Sociological Review*, xliii, 1950, and xliii, 1951, and in *Public Administration* xxix, Winter 1951).

doned; but as the crisis nears, it seems that a new activity in which the whole village can collaborate is started. Therefore, as the brass band failed, a choir was founded; as the choir failed, a football club was started; when that began to fail, an annual carnival was instituted.

Dr. Frankenberg himself observed only the transition from football club to carnival, and he tentatively advances the more general hypothesis on the basis of what villagers told him about the past. But his tentative analysis convinces me; and I see in his analysis a most significant contribution to general theories about social life. Other observers have noted this failure of a succession of village activities. They have also noted the tendency, present in Pentrediwaith, for positions of authority in village clubs to be held by persons in the so-called 'upper classes'. They have concluded that both these sets of facts show a lack of interest in these activities on the part of villagers, and an inability of villagers to organize for themselves. Thus an informant whom Mr. Williams placed in the 'upper-upper class' told him: 'I can't recall any movement in the village [Gosforth] that ever had any success unless someone of the so-called higher class took an interest.'[1] This may indeed be true of Gosforth; but in Pentrediwaith at least, it is not lack of interest on the part of the villagers that has led to the failure of 'movements', but rather too much interest. And though here, too, 'upper class people' and 'strangers' appear as presidents and chairmen (partly to obtain their subscriptions), Dr. Frankenberg shows that they are led rather than leaders. For when a crisis is reached, one of these higher-class people, or a stranger to the village, is thrust into the position of appearing to take the decision which forces one party out of the current activity; and gossip can blame this person for destroying village unity: 'We would be happy if foreigners did not make trouble!'

Dr. Frankenberg compares this use of persons who live outside the ordinary round of village life with similar institutions in Africa—the position of Nuer leopard-skin chiefs as mediators in feuds, using of oracular verdicts in family quarrels among the Tallensi, and the like. In making this comparison, he advances a theory of how the existence of a village community is possible. For inevitably in the village, within its members'

[1] *op. cit.*, p. 126.

acceptance of their unity, there are animosities between cliques, sects, kindreds, occupational groups, individuals. He shows how these are fed into the recreational activity, which village opinion and pressure insist shall be of interest to everyone. Taking up Dr. Elizabeth Colson's brilliant exposition of the role of gossip in a modern Red Indian community,[1] he exhibits how these struggles are rarely fought openly in committee, but how differences of opinion concealing them work out in behind-the-back tattle, gossip and scandal; many villagers who are in fact at loggerheads can outwardly maintain a show of harmony and friendship. In a crisis, as we have seen, the 'stranger' takes the blame. Many devices—such as forgetting to record minutes—secure this anonymity in dispute. The end result is that the village remains a village, for the values of unity pass into the new activity: it is a village activity. After each failure the villagers feel that they can make a fresh start, with old difficulties purged with the failing activity. They see their difficulties as arising from the football, rather than the football as involved in their differences.

Anthropologists will see some similarity between the 'ceremonial symbolism' of these recreational activities and the structure of ceremonies in tribal society. There too, some ceremonies, in their dance and mime and other rites, exhibit certain standardized conflicts within the group which performs the rites, while at the same time stressing that these conflicts exist within an overall acceptance of common values and goals, and of the group's unity. The ceremonies involve prescribed actions in which the actors have to behave as if they felt the animosities which they enact. And they are performed under the believed control of ancestral spirits or gods.[2] Yet these ceremonies are long-established social mechanisms which have become set in custom. Perhaps we can see the process by which they developed in the history of Pentrediwaith's football club.

The hypothesis receives support from a whole series of novels about the life of small communities. At the end of *South Wind's*

[1] *The Makah Indians*, Manchester University Press, 1953.
[2] I have lately myself made explicit this anthropological thesis from recent fieldwork in Africa, in *Rituals of Rebellion in South-East Africa*, Manchester University Press, 1954, and *Custom and Conflict in Africa*, Blackwell, 1955.

crisis even Signor Malapizzo and the Church were reconciled within Nepenthean unity. Margery Sharp's *The Stone of Chastity* ends the turmoil caused by an egregious anthropologist with a demonstration of the virtue of the village's women, even when the virtue of almost every female could be doubted by at least one man; the reputation of the community could not be assailed. And the assault of an almost equally egregious anthropologist on the values of an Irish village ends, after a similar crisis, in a demonstration of village unity and virtue in Honor Tracy's *The Straight and Narrow Path*. The idea is undoubtedly implicit in several novels: it is something new to have it made into an explicit thesis as in this book.

Dr. Frankenberg hesitated to state his theory as strongly as I have done, because he does not believe that the cycle of one symbolically unifying, recreational activity after another is the only social process at work. It appeared to him that there was proceeding within this cycle a process of increasing failure of interest in these activities, and hence an increasing failure to run the activities successfully. The younger people are cajoled and compelled by their elders with growing difficulty to take an interest; and the elders themselves grow less interested. Of course, the young feel the pull of 'home', and in middle age they may cajole their own children. But Dr. Frankenberg concludes that the day may soon come when these activities can no longer be run, and his judgment is that then the village will cease to be 'a village' as a community and become a collocation of houses whose inhabitants go out to work in the nearby towns. Hence his stress on the fact that he is describing 'a village without work' (*Pentrediwaith* is his *nom-de-village*). For he suggests that the situation would be different in an African village whose members are united in common productive activities and consume their products together, or in an English village where the men all worked for local employers. Indeed, one of our colleagues grew up in such a village, and told us that recreations were differently organized, while Dr. Frankenberg himself found quite a different situation in a South Wales village he studied for University College, Cardiff. The argument that Pentrediwaith is a village whose men leave each day to work in scattered places, while their womenfolk remain at home in the village, is basic to the whole analysis.

Many people are concerned to develop community life in the new towns and the housing estates which are being built. For the feeling that people get happiness out of living in good neighbourly communities is strong in Britain, as elsewhere. This feeling appeared in the appreciative mirth with which cinema audiences responded to the way that the Scottish island in *Whiskey Galore* and the English village in *The Titfield Thunderbolt* outwitted by their unity the soulless bureaucrats and business-men of the nation; and Ealing Studios in *Passport to Pimlico* and *The Galloping Major* even created in London itself little com-munities, which were similarly united against the impersonality of the outside world. But we know that the problems of creating a community life are difficult: the difficulties are illuminated in this story of the struggle against English indus-trialism of a small village, proud in the traditions of Wales, isolated in its beautiful valley, united in kinship and sentiment but divided into cliques and sects and individuals.

For Dr. Frankenberg tells the story of a struggle to survive as a community against the pressure of the outside world, and against the enticement of amusements open to individuals alone. He tells the story sympathetically, for I do not believe he conceals where his own feelings lie. Inevitably some of the things that the villagers do appear to be laughable foibles, and he has written of these foibles humorously—but always generously. He has concealed the village from outsiders under the name Pentrediwaith: I do not believe it was necessary, for no one could fail to sympathize with the villagers. In addition, even if we find amusement in the doings of Pentrediwaith people, it will be a wry amusement. For this analysis has lessons for us all: I certainly recognized in the intrigues on the football committee actions I had seen in student societies, in govern-mental departments, and in university organization.

For a social anthropologist the interest of this book lies in its application of ideas developed in the study of tribal society to a community in Britain. And, as I write, this is the first full published study of this kind since Arensberg and Kimball's work on County Clare twenty years ago. Since then, 'tradi-tional' social anthropology has advanced considerably: and I consider that Dr. Frankenberg's use of our recent analyses of community life, with all its conflicts, of feud and its mediators,

of the role of ceremonial, etc., is most illuminating. More than
this, he suggests for me new lines of analysis in our traditional
field. I believe too, despite the limitations of our methods, his
study will be useful to sociologists, political scientists, and other
students of British life.

But over and above its academic value, this is a book with
insight and wit to interest anyone: for it brings a new kind of
systematic order into a story that is seemingly known to us all.

MAX GLUCKMAN

Department of Social Anthropology,
    Victoria University of Manchester,
December, 1956

I

PENTREDIWAITH

PENTREDIWAITH is a civil parish in a North Wales valley. If one enters this valley by the most ancient route over the mountain, as I did the first time that I went there, one can stand on a ridge at right angles to the road near the church and look down on the village of Pentrediwaith. It seems a compact unit, a community, isolated in the elbow of a steep-sided valley. Great hills of slate-refuse give the impression that it is a slate-mining community. One sees two disused mills on the outskirts. If one follows the road down to the village to the crossroads at its centre one comes to three more roads. Two of these lead up into the hills again to places from which, once more, Pentrediwaith can be seen as a compact geographical unit. The third leads downwards and outwards from the Welsh hills into the Shropshire plain and into England.

In the chapters that follow I am principally concerned with discussing certain aspects of the social life of this village. The village seen from the air or from the hills looks like an isolated community; villagers feel that it is isolated. They also consider that it ought to be a united community and behave as if it were. The network of kinship and acquaintanceship in which all have their places, and the family solidarity which has grown out of Pentrediwaith's history, confirm villagers in their view. But in fact their isolation is in most senses an illusion. Geographically, economically and historically, the village is part of a larger whole.

Geographically, it is a village in a valley which contains other villages. A river passes through them all and they are linked by a system of roads which connect Castell at the foot of the valley with Glyndafad at its head. Castell, on the fringes of English industrial culture, is linked by the main

9

road with Glyndafad on the borders of the Welsh sheep-farming culture of the Mid-Wales hills. The hills which surround
Pentrediwaith contain rock which has, in the past, proved
commercially valuable; slate has been mined here and granite
quarried. Many years ago there was a silica works. The mills
on the outskirts of the village were, until only a few years ago,
links in the chain by which Welsh wool from Berwyn flocks
was converted into Bradford woollens for distribution throughout England and the world.

These natural resources and the industries to which they
gave rise were responsible for the growth of the population of
the village. Together with this growth they made necessary
the roads joining the village with Castell and Bigtown, and the
small-gauge railway which until the 1930's took the products
of Pentrediwaith's mines and quarries to Castell and the main
railway line. These developments also brought people to the
village from the outside. 'Outsiders' today play an important
part in maintaining community life.

The economy that was built on local material resources is
now a thing of the past. The economic basis of Pentrediwaith
village community is gone. The villagers still reside together
in their compact nuclear settlement, but many no longer work
in the valley alongside their fellow-villagers. The roads, built
to take Pentrediwaith's products to a wider market, now serve
to carry the men of the village to their daily work outside the
valley and, if not right outside Wales, outside Welsh-speaking
areas. The quarries brought Pentrediwaith men into daily
contact with men from Melin, and Pentrenesaf, and other
villages and hamlets within the valley. Now they work as
labourers on building sites and as hands in factories, side by
side not only with people of the valley, but with Englishmen,
Irishmen, and even Poles drawn from a wide area of North
Wales and Shropshire. This situation means that the men of
Pentrediwaith, although they continue to live in the village,
spend their working days away from it. Through their 'foreign'
workmates they develop interests outside the village and Wales
which are only partially shared by their womenfolk;[1] for the

[1] This is of course a generally recognized feature of industrial societies
everywhere. Compare, for example, Whyte, W. F., *Human Relations in the*
Restaurant Industry, New York, 1948, p. 131: 'Wherever people work

women still remain tied to the village both by residence and by their work. This provides a major division in village social life which I shall discuss in detail.

The most important feature of Pentrediwaith's lack of isolation is the fact that, historically and socially, Pentrediwaith is a part of a much larger society—England and Wales. This statement is not a mere platitude nor a mechanical geographical truism. Pentrediwaith does not just happen to be in Wales, it is an organic part of Welsh society. The economic and social class divisions of Wales are reflected in the social life of Pentrediwaith, and the class divisions which arose in the course of the internal development of Pentrediwaith play their part in determining the social structure of the whole of England and Wales.

In Pentrediwaith and elsewhere some divisions are more fundamental than others. People divided by them are seldom linked across them by any uniting ties. This has been especially true in Wales, where for long periods of its history English and Welsh have been almost synonymous with landlord and tenant or capital and labour. Disraeli's description of employers and employed as two nations applied literally to Wales.[1] In Pentrediwaith, and I believe in other parts of rural Wales, this division is shown very clearly when the present-day constitution of the Parish Council is compared with that of the County Council, Rural District Council and, especially, the Bench of Magistrates. To consider only the extreme cases of the Bench and the Parish Council (discussed in Chapter III), we find that the members of each body look to different sources not only for their income but also for their whole social life. In general the Bench are salaried or self-employed, English-speaking and Anglican. They do not take an active part in the daily life of

---

together, they cease to be separate isolated individuals and organise themselves as groups of friends. . . . The importance of the social relations growing out of the job can hardly be overestimated. The Committee on Human Relations in Industry studies of city districts in Chicago show that the city neighbourhood is becoming steadily less important as a centre for the social life of its people. Many working people interviewed told us that they made their friends in their places of work.'

See also Kuper, L., *Living in Towns*, Cresset Press, 1953.

[1] See Williams, C. R., 'The Welsh Religious Revival, 1904-05,' *British Journal of Sociology*, 3, 1952.

any one village, although they are drawn as vice-presidents and presidents into the surface life of many villages both within and outside the valley. They completely lack ties of kinship with the people of the village and the valley. They do not even live in the village but in big houses on the outskirts or at a distance.

The parish councillors on the other hand are wage-earners, Welsh-speaking and Nonconformist. Their whole life is oriented towards village society and their contact even with other villages in the valley is slight. They are Chapel deacons and society secretaries, but only within the one village. Although no one of them is directly related to any other, each has his place in the complicated network of kinship and affinity which unites most of the village residents to each other. Most parish councillors live in the village itself and on the housing estate.[1]

The division between the social class represented by magistrates and the class represented by parish councillors is stated here in absolute terms, but will be modified in later chapters. It is almost, but not quite, congruent with the distinction between 'outsiders' and 'Pentre people'. It is a division which has arisen out of the economic and social life of the village itself. The outsiders, again generally speaking, come in contact with the villagers only as employers or in other positions of authority such as magistrates. But they are known personally to villagers, who treat them with friendliness tinged with respect. Such outsiders contribute to village funds and help the villagers in other ways. In 1953 class antagonism was often overshadowed by personal friendliness. This has not, of course, always been the case, as even a cursory reading of Welsh history demonstrates. Thus a correspondent of *The Times* wrote in 1843:

> It cannot be denied that the people look upon the landlords and gentry and Magistrates, as a *class*, with hatred and suspicion, and if one quarter of the stories are true which I have heard, not without just cause.[2]

Landlords and magistrates 'as a class' are still distrusted and looked upon with suspicion. At the Parish Councils Association

[1] Cf. Mitchell, G. D., 'The Parish Council and the Rural Community,' *Public Administration* XXIX; and discussion in Brennan, T., *et al.*, *Social Change in South-West Wales*, Watts, 1954, ch. VI.

[2] *The Times*, 30 September, 1843, quoted in *Report of The Royal Commission on Land in Wales and Monmouthshire*, 1893-96, p. 156.

meeting which I describe they were attacked as a class. Within Pentrediwaith, however, where their power is now in any case very limited, even the remains of suspicion usually (but not always) gives way to liking based on personal experience. There was a sharper division between the villagers and those who, although they had originated from amongst Pentre people, had prospered economically and were trying to renounce the informal social ties that identified them with the mass of Pentre people.

The class division between parish councillors themselves and participants in the other organs of local government is emphasized in the minds of both the parish councillors and Pentre people in general by the fact that the Parish Council, which represents most closely their interests as wage-earners and as the inhabitants of a particular local area, is almost powerless to change conditions. Pentre people feel that only the Parish Council has a true appreciation of village problems. This feeling is further emphasized by the fact that the Rural District Council and the County Council, which are remote from both a particular locality and the common people, are invested with power which Pentre villagers have often resented even when it was, in fact, operating to their advantage.

The position of the Parish Council as a body is interesting in another respect. Many if not all of the social activities which are carried on within Pentrediwaith are imposed upon the village by formal or informal pressures which arise outside the village. This applies with equal force to recreation and to politics. Thus Pentrediwaith chose football as its sport because of the existing framework of Football Associations in the county and the nation. Villagers organized Coronation festivities in emulation of, and in competition with, other villages, and after consultation at the county level between parish councils and the higher bodies. Pentre people found it no hardship to organize Coronation festivities, but there are other tasks imposed upon them as individuals and as groups which they do not welcome. The County Council makes decisions which affect villagers and which they do not like. The task of interpreting such higher decisions and advocating their adoption falls on the Parish Council. Thus, at least in the restricted field of administration, the Parish Council 'articulates the parish with a wider social system',[1] and like all persons, corporate or individual, in this position, it faces both ways. On the one hand it supports the villagers against the county authorities, on the other villagers see it as imposing county decisions upon them. Although occasions on which the Parish Council actually had to enforce unpopular higher decisions could not arise, villagers erroneously see local government as a hierarchy.[2]

The divisions that I have so far considered, those between Pentre people and outsiders, wage-earners and the salaried or self-employed, arise out of the existing social structure of the village. They are, in sociological terms, divisions within the system. But even these divisions are bridged by some informal ties which link individuals across them. There are, however, other social divisions in Pentrediwaith which are bequeathed to the internal system by divisions derived from the external system in which Pentrediwaith exists. These are the attributes which in the course of Welsh history have become identified with the 'national' class divisions of Wales. They have already been mentioned in defining the characteristics of magistrates and parish councillors. They are Church and Chapel; and English-speaking and Welsh-speaking. Since even class divisions which have their origin in Pentrediwaith are not marked by invariable mutual hostility and segregation, it is not surprising that on the village level national schisms are bridged across by innumerable formal and informal ties.[3] Pentre people, within fairly narrow limits, belong to the same economic class, but they are divided and united by group loyalties bequeathed to them by their own history and by the history and social structure of the larger society of which they form a part.

In the past the Anglican Church—the name 'Church *of* England *in* Wales' reveals its history—first antagonized the

[1] Barnes, J. A., 'Class and Committees in a Norwegian Island Parish', *Human Relations*, vii, 1954, 1, p. 53.

[2] This 'ambivalent' position of institutions within hierarchies is familiar to social anthropologists. See Barnes, J. A., Gluckman, M., and Mitchell, J. C., 'The Village Headman in British Central Africa', in *Africa*, xxix, 1949.

[3] Compare the attitude of the Makah to whites, in and outside the reservation, reported by Colson, E., *The Makah Indians*, Manchester, 1953, ch. iv, pp. 88 *et seq.*

Welsh people by its attitude to the Welsh language. Later, when this had been at least partially remedied, it was still identified with the class interests of the landlords, who were mostly English or anglicized. The Nonconformist movement, although it also had its first origins in England, overcame the handicap of its birth by its championship of both the Welsh language and the common people of Wales. By 1953, the Church in Pentrediwaith had services in Welsh alternating with its English ones, and had a Welsh-speaking Vicar. It still catered for 'outsiders' both rich and poor, but also for nearly a third of the ordinary villagers. Many of these Church-going Pentre people differed from their neighbours only because they attended Church instead of Chapel and sent their children to Church Sunday and day schools. Sometimes they did no more than say, when they were asked, that they were Church. Church and Chapel people were to be found in the same families united by intermarriage. The Baptist Minister and the Anglican Vicar jointly officiated at some funerals, and on national occasions such as Armistice Day.[1]

Nevertheless, there remains an underlying hostility between Church people as a group and Chapel people as a group. In times of stress and in crises when decisions have to be made, this hostility sometimes comes into the open. One such occasion is described below. Even in this, an open dispute on the future education of the children of both groups, there was no real doctrinal split. Neither Church nor Chapel people had cause for concern about the spiritual fate of their children. In the dispute the Chapel people were content with the existing arrangements for the early school years of their children. They were opposed to a suggested moving of the infants of both Church and Chapel to the Church-school buildings. They complained of the age of these buildings and wanted to let things be. But the Church people felt that an attack on their school buildings was an attack on the Church. Neither side objected on doctrinal grounds to the Church and Chapel school-children being taught together; the matter was never discussed in these terms. It became a conflict between Church people and Chapel people with

---

[1] This appears to be a common state of affairs in Britain. See Stewart, C., *The Village Surveyed*, Arnold, 1948, p. 86.

The circle indicates the area on the English-Welsh border within which
the village of Pentrediwaith lies.

undertones of English-Welsh hostility. The actual substance of the dispute became obscured by social divisions, the existence of which normally remains hidden beneath the surface of village life.

Church and Chapel people are normally united not only by kinship links between the groups but by common residence and common social and economic interests. They support one another's social events and in activities like football and the carnival the Church-Chapel division is of no account. It is forgotten and replaced by others based on family feuds and sex differences. Of the two main village drama groups, which had originally been one but had split on a personal quarrel, one was identified with Church and the other with Chapel. But Chapel and Church personnel combined in both and villagers attended both sets of performances. When the Church group's play failed to come up to expectations, Chapel villagers were more critical than Church-goers were. Church people found reasons for the failure which Chapel members were not interested in seeking. But the village did not divide into hostile camps on the issue.

During the last decades of the nineteenth century and the first decades of the twentieth, before the Church in Wales was disestablished and disendowed, it is probable that there was, even in Pentrediwaith, a real and unbridgeable division between Anglican and Nonconformist. Today the situation in the village is more complex. The intermingling of groups is exemplified by one village couple of which the husband is Scots Baptist and the wife Church. Their children attend the Council school in the week and the Baptist Sunday school. They themselves attend the Church. Another couple, mixed Calvinistic Methodist and Baptist, send their children to the Church school in the week but to the Baptist Sunday school. Although Baptists, the dominant village religious group, tend to shop at Baptist shops, ties of neighbourhood and close friendship link individuals across denominational boundaries. When, some years ago, a Church family lost all their belongings in a fire, the committee which collected a large sum for them in the village included three Chapel members out of its total four.

In another village in Wales, with which I have a superficial acquaintance, and which has been harder hit by emigration than Pentrediwaith, the Chapel people contributed as much as, if not more than, the Church people to the Church-in-Wales appeal. At harvest festivals in this village not only does the same congregation attend the services in the Church and the Chapel, but the hymns in both are accompanied by the same organist. In Pentrediwaith unity has not been pressed so far, but in village conditions open and continuous breach is not possible. If it did occur it would place in conflict not only friends but different members of the same family. Thus 'national' divisions are at village level modified by the face-to-face character of village society.

Despite the cross-linkages between groups there is always a danger that their mutual hostility may awaken. The attempt to avoid such open conflicts which disrupt social relations within the village is a very marked feature of social life in Pentrediwaith. This has several minor effects on the day-to-day behaviour of villagers. Thus Pentre people rarely give the lie direct to statements made in public, or even to those made in private by people with whom they are not on very intimate terms. Villagers rarely refuse a request but delay indefinitely fulfilling one of which they disapprove. Minutes of committees are kept in very little detail, if they are kept at all; no discussion is recorded and even the names of proposer and seconder are omitted from the record of decisions made. Committees of the village, like the village itself, must maintain an appearance of impersonal, unanimous, even leaderless unity.

But this attempt to avoid awakening dormant hostilities also has a major consequence in the social life of the village. 'Strangers' (who are not necessarily 'outsiders') are brought into an activity to take the responsibility and withstand the unpopularity of leadership and the taking of decisions. The role of strangers in this respect will be a constantly recurring theme in the chapters that follow. The importance of strangers in village life is not, in my view, a pathological sign of the decay of community life, nor an indication that villagers are not capable of running their own affairs.[1] Decisions are usually in fact taken by the villagers themselves. They only *appear* to

---

[1] Cf. Whiteley and Curle who imply this in their works cited in the Bibliography.

be made by strangers who are forced to shoulder the responsibility for decisions when they prove unpopular with dissident
groups of villagers. Such 'strangers' may be complete outsiders
to the category of Pentre people, or they may be drawn from
deviant individuals and groups within this category. Thus
while it is possible to count the number of outsiders who participate in village activity, one cannot count the number of
strangers. 'Strangers' is a shifting concept, and a stranger in
one context is not a stranger in another. During 1953 there
were occasions when even I was not regarded as a stranger, and
others when a village woman, a Welsh-speaking and Nonconformist member of a village family, was so regarded because
she had spent her childhood in another village of the valley.
The 'stranger' chairman of one women's committee owed his
strangeness to the fact that he was a man 'leading' (or perhaps
being led by) a group of women.

Conflict in the village cannot always be avoided despite
these social mechanisms. Disputes do come into the open at
public meetings and during formal committee discussions.
When they do, they often result in the resignation, not merely
of an individual, but of an informal group of his supporters as
well. The football club in 1954 finally reached the stage when
it was in feud with most of the village women and with so
many of the village men that it had no support left. From what
villagers told me, I concluded that the male voice choir and
the brass band had perished for similar reasons. It seems to
me possible that there is a sort of cycle of public activities
which rise and fall in this way. Unfortunately, I have not
sufficient historical material to verify this hypothesis.

I have so far been discussing communal activities and the
role within them of certain social divisions in village society.
These are associated with classes and their cultural accretions
in the nation-wide system of which Pentrediwaith is one small
part. There is, however, another major division which cuts
across all others in Pentrediwaith. This is the division between
'The Men' and 'The Women'. Since Pentrediwaith lost the
economic basis of its community existence this division has
become very important, for although most of the village men
go away from the valley to work, the women remain at home.
The informal ties of friendship which used to unite men who

worked together in the quarry now only survive in a few isolated groups. Examples are the few coalminers of the village and the farmers who still recognize their common interests and in some situations act as groups. The majority of village men, like men in industrial areas elsewhere, no longer work side by side with their residential neighbours.[1] The women of course still do, and despite the extraordinary care with which they clean their houses and look after their children, they find time for gossip and discussion amongst themselves. They drop in on each other informally for cups of tea and meet while shopping in the village. They also work together in sewing groups and work-parties preparing material for sales-of-work or village entertainments. At such groups they discuss village affairs and reach their own conclusions on the proper course of action in any particular situation. They enforce their point of view both by informal pressure on their husbands and by their concerted efforts at public meetings to which the men have the disadvantage of coming unprepared. The influence of the women in the running of purely recreational events in the village is obvious. It is also greater in the decision of public matters than is apparent on the surface.

The gossip, and to some extent 'backbiting', of the women is not limited in its functions to uniting the women as a group against the men and making women's voices more effective in village counsels. Gossip, even malicious gossip, has not necessarily the pathological significance ascribed to it by some sociologists.[2] On the contrary, as Dr. Colson points out, gossip may be of great importance in maintaining a sense of community. It provides in Pentrediwaith another criterion which helps to distinguish Pentre people from outsiders. Pentre people are those whom other Pentre people gossip with and about. Nor, of course, is gossip confined to women. In the farms the wives seldom leave the farmhouses, yet they are often among the best informed people in the village on local affairs. Their husbands, who go into the village daily, provide them with the news. In other village homes the husband, although away

[1] See Kuper, L., *Living in Towns*, London, 1953, pp. 118-20; Whyte, W. F., *op. cit.*, and Homans, G., *The Human Group*, ch. xiii.

[2] See Curle, A., 'What Happened to Three Villages' in *The Listener*, 18 December, 1952; Whiteley, W., 'Littletown-in-Overspill' in Kuper, *op. cit.*

all day, receives the daily news from his wife while he eats his evening meal. Villagers pride themselves on knowing all about their immediate neighbours and, indeed, all other villagers, but they take little or no interest in the personal affairs of 'outsiders'. Villagers could rarely do more than name the English owners of weekend and holiday bungalows, and often could not even do that. Such people were referred to, if at all, eponymously, as 'Mrs. Morgan's visitor' or by the names of the houses in which they lived. Villagers did not hesitate to make accusations against and ridicule their friends and relatives, but outsiders were not allowed this privilege. Even my mildest criticisms were cut short with such remarks as: 'That's my cousin you're talking about'. On specific occasions I was rebuked for mildly criticizing distant cousins, and once for commenting adversely on the whist-playing of my hearer's prospective son-in-law's grandmother.

Gossip was also used as a vehicle through which criticism and conflicts could be expressed without ripening into open hostility. Private gossip was in a sense a licensed method of airing public grievances in private. Only when such grievances were brought into the open and publicly revealed, usually by strangers, did open hostility occur. Thus gossip critical of personal behaviour was not an effective means of social control. The discussion of adultery and 'living tally'[1] had apparently no effect upon the culprits. Save that no one commits suicide in Pentre because he has fathered an illegitimate child, Malinowski's account of the Trobriand attitude to breaches of exogamy accurately describes villagers' tolerant attitude to breaches of the sexual code:

> If the affair is carried on *sub rosa* with a certain amount of decorum, and if no one in particular stirs up trouble, 'public opinion' will gossip, but not demand any harsh punishment. If, on the contrary, scandal breaks out, everyone turns against the guilty pair and by ostracism or insults one or the other may be driven to suicide.[2]

In Pentrediwaith estrangement or public confession and apology in the Chapel takes the place of suicide.

[1] This term is used locally for what is more formally known as 'living in sin'.
[2] Malinowski, B., *Crime and Custom in Savage Society*, London, 1926, p. 80.

C

Even when public confession does not take place, 'the village' knows well who are the fathers of particular illegitimate children, and who is 'carrying on' with whom. Knowledge of this kind about their neighbours and their families, and participation, even as enemies, in group conflicts within the village bind the people of Pentrediwaith more closely into their community. For despite the many factors which divide Pentre people from each other, and despite the collapse of the village economy, Pentrediwaith is still regarded by its people as a community. Within this community, Pentre people live in households in the village; and their friends, neighbours and relatives live nearby. Households are linked by kinship and other loyalties and divided by quarrels. These links and divisions are reflected in the wider social life of the village and will be discussed in my analysis of the football and carnival disputes below. Quarrels, loyalties, knowledge of one another's background and lives, and the past and present sharing of mutual experiences in good and bad times, unite them in the knowledge that they are Pentre people and that, even if they go to live elsewhere, Pentrediwaith is their home.

In the chapters that follow the lines of analysis suggested in this introduction will be followed up. In Chapter II I shall first try to place Pentrediwaith in its context as part of Wales and then give some indication of the main features of its historical, social, and economic development. Chapter III is intended to give such information about the general characteristics of present-day Pentrediwaith as is necessary for the understanding of Chapters IV and V. In Chapter III some of my material on basic social divisions will be presented in a preliminary way. In Chapters IV and V some specific social situations and institutions will be discussed with special reference to the role of social classes and other divisions in the making of decisions, and to the part played in this process by 'strangers'.

II

THE VILLAGE COMMUNITY

THE VILLAGE

THERE are many kinds of social organization in Wales, and even the Dafad valley itself is not homogeneous from one end to the other. Nor is Pentrediwaith isolated from the rest of the valley. At the head of the valley is the hamlet of Glyndafad, embedded in the hills. Sheep-farming is its major occupation and it is not far removed in culture or terrain from the parish of Llanfihangel-yng-Ngwynfa described by Alwyn Rees in his book, *Life in a Welsh Countryside*. Welsh is the only language spoken by the people of Glyndafad even to English-speaking villagers of Pentrediwaith. But even here there is a hotel which is popular with tourists and some of the hill farms have been bought by Englishmen who farm them themselves.

Only in 1953, when I had already arrived in Pentrediwaith, was a regular daily bus service from Glyndafad to Bigtown introduced, enabling Glyndafad men to join other inhabitants of the valley in industry if they wished. Two other hamlets between Glyndafad and Pentrediwaith used to provide labour to quarries on the way to Pentre as well as to farms on the way to Glyndafad. Pentrediwaith itself was until recently a quarrying village, but also contained wool factories and provided a centre for sheep and wool sales for the valley farmers. Like other quarrying areas it was a stronghold of Welsh culture, of which its poets and other *Eisteddfodwyr* were the outward signs. It maintains some of these characteristics still despite the closing of local industry, and the integration of its menfolk into the factory economy of local large towns. Castell, at the foot of the valley and on the English border, is on a main road and on the railway. It is entirely English-speaking, despite its coal mine, and transport to centres of secondary industry is frequent and comparatively inexpensive.

It is true that English influence can be felt more easily here on the border, but the area has been on the border for centuries and it is only now, under the influence of industrial change, that English behaviour, language, and custom have become a real threat to the survival of the Welsh language and culture of ordinary people in the valley. Williams in his *History of Modern Wales* states the case more generally:

Besides, industrialism linked Wales with England as never before in its history. While Wales was isolated geographically, and was almost self-sufficing economically, the influence of England was not strong. But the building of roads and railways, and the enormous growth of Welsh industry as part of the economic development of Britain, profoundly affected Welsh life; so much so that there is a marked tendency to regard Welsh culture as being in essence the culture of rural Wales and not of the industrial centres.

This does not mean that there was no English influence at all in the Dafad valley. Here as elsewhere in Wales, the landowning class has long been English or anglicized. In mediaeval times the valley was in one of the principalities of the kingdom of Powys in North-Eastern Wales. The last Welsh prince to rule the whole principality died in A.D. 1269. His successor's lands were sequestrated by the king of England and granted in 1282 to Roger Mortimer, who is described as having soon after 'ruled all Wales like a king'. The valley, and the parish of Pentrediwaith within it, have been dominated by its minority of Englishmen or anglicized Welsh gentry ever since. By the end of the fourteenth century Welsh traditional tenure survived only in the names of the land divisions. Some of these proper names survive still. The inhabitants were then, and remained until the nineteenth century, tenants of the holder of the local large estate.

This estate was divided in the early nineteenth century and most of Pentrediwaith eventually passed into the hands of a Lancashire ironmaster and coalowner. His grandson sold this smaller estate in 1952 to the tenant farmers and for forestry development. The Hall stood empty in 1953. Until after the second world war the holders of the Hall and of the remains of the larger estate acted as squires not only to their own tenants but to the whole village. In the 'twenties, for example, when an

heir was born to the Squire, the whole village was invited to
the celebration at the Hall, which is situated in a hamlet on
the mountain side within the parish. Buses were provided to
take villagers there and back. Another party was promised
for the son's coming of age, but the last war and its aftermath
prevented this from taking place. The birthday celebration
thirty years ago was the only occasion on which most of the
villagers had ever visited this hamlet.

The departure from the village of the landed gentry left a
vacancy in social life which is partly filled by tradesmen and
other 'outsiders'. In Pentrediwaith the gentry were not removed
by the will or action of the people but by external circumstances. For this reason leaders were not created in the course
of a struggle 'to throw off the yoke', and each social situation
which arises in Pentrediwaith finds the villagers without
leadership. The devices used to overcome this handicap will
be discussed in detail below.

The Dafad valley lay on the borders of several great estates,
but by the time of the register in 1842 there were already many
owner occupiers in the parish, and new industrial powers
were arising in the valley. Quarries and fulling-mills were
established very early, at least by the fifteenth century. Quarrying expanded and became well established in the eighteenth
and nineteenth centuries. By the beginning of the twentieth
century Pentrediwaith itself had a granite quarry and flannel
mills in addition to the slate mine. The village grew in the
second half of the nineteenth century, as Bethesda, Festiniog
and other towns in Snowdonia had grown in the first half.
Dodd writes:

In all the chief quarrying districts the decade following
the repeal of the slate duty (i.e. 1831-41) seems to have been
the period of most rapid growth. The population of
Caernarvonshire increased during those years by 22 per
cent.—almost twice as high a rate as in any other county
of North Wales; and most of this growth is directly attribut-
able to slate. The quarrying population was forming its
own villages—new Nonconformist parishes, as it were, each
clustering round and many of them named after the first
chapel to be erected. The Penrhyn workmen found Lord
Penrhyn's model houses too far away, and they built homes

for themselves round Bethesda Chapel, just at the foot of
the quarry; by the 'sixties Bethesda had five or six thousand
inhabitants. In Llanberis parish the old village was left
high and dry; a new Llanberis arose on the southern side
of Llyn Padarn, and an Ebenezer further north in Llandein-
iolen parish; and colonies of workmen from Cilgwyn straggled
all over the wild mountain lands of Llandwrog and Llan-
llyfni parishes.

Some of the villages and hamlets, as we have seen, had
been put up by the quarrymen themselves, on common land
in their spare time. Similar developments were taking place
at Festiniog. The population of the parish was only 732
when the first census was taken and it did not exceed a
thousand till 1821. By 1831 it was over 1,600 and in the
next ten years it almost doubled itself; a quarter of the
inhabitants were registered in 1841 as born outside the
county. Then there was a pause, to be followed by still
more striking growth in the 'sixties and 'seventies. But it
was not in the existing village that the new houses were
run up; a new village—Blaenau Festiniog—built of solid
slabs of slate, had come into existence in the north of the
parish, close by the principal quarries.[1]

The difficulties of transport at Pentrediwaith made it rise
later than the Caernarvon quarrying villages, and its decline
was both earlier and more rapid. In the 1870's a tramway to
carry away the slate from Pentrediwaith was authorized by
Act of Parliament and built. The population increased and the
village grew; and until the 1920's Pentrediwaith, at least when
considered in relation to the surrounding countryside, flourished
and prospered.

After the General Strike of 1926 and the depression of the
'thirties village prosperity declined with the national crisis.
The tramway ceased to operate and was dismantled in 1935.
Men left the village to seek work and the unmarried women
went to Liverpool and Manchester to work as resident domes-
tics. By taking the men away to serve in the forces, or as directed
labour elsewhere, the war of 1939-45 temporarily solved
Pentrediwaith's difficulties. The rule of the squire had its final
fling in the Home Guard. Finally, between 1946 and 1952,
village industry died completely. One by one the quarries of

[1] Dodd, A. H., *The Industrial Revolution in North Wales*, p. 219.

slate and stone and the factories closed down. Many of the
neighbouring farms were bought by Englishmen. The large
estates finally dissolved. In 1953 virtually the only jobs left in
the village were for Council roadmen and postmen. The men
travelled daily to work in the nearby towns or to building
sites. Many men have moved from one building job to another
since the quarries closed. When the present building projects
end unemployment is expected.

This, very briefly, is the background of the economic history
of Pentrediwaith. The memory of past prosperity (often
exaggerated in recollection) and the fear of future unemployment, together with the unpleasant necessity of a journey
away to work, dominated the social life of Pentrediwaith in
1953. Houses have been built in Pentrediwaith since the war,
and this provides a reason for staying there despite its lack of
work and the social isolation which the young men and women
often complain about. In addition to this reason, there is
another conflict in the mind of a would-be emigrant. Even if
all the economic arguments make him wish to leave, there is
an attachment to the village and its people to be overcome.
Even the emigrant family does not cut all ties. During 1953,
for example, there was a number of funerals of people born in
the village who had lived for many years in South Wales and
parts of England. One Australian ex-villager returned on a
visit after a forty-year absence. Another recent emigrant to
Australia broadcast from Sydney on the Welsh Home Service.
Families who have only gone as far as Manchester or Birming-
ham are visited and return the visits. Men and girls who go
away to work live at the houses of other villagers who went
before them, or if none can be found, they go to the homes of
fellow Baptists or Methodists.

This attachment to home or place of birth is not, of course,
limited to Pentrediwaith, or even to Wales. It is, however, a
very noticeable feature of Welsh culture. It will be remembered
that the three major events of the Royal National Eisteddfod
are the Chairing and Crowning ceremonies and the welcome
to returned exiles. The Chair itself is usually provided by an
'exiled' Welshman.

In Pentrediwaith this attachment is much stronger among
the women than the men. Several men have told me in con-

versation on the point that they wanted to leave in the 1930's but their wives would not agree. One man had a job and a house waiting for him, but he said his wife would not go— 'she wanted to be with her relations'. Women have also told me how their husbands have pressed them to leave but they have wanted to stay in the village. This sort of attachment to the village and to the valley is partly a function of Chapel and kin-group membership. The village is where Pentre people belong, elsewhere they would be strangers. This is particularly true of the women, who are less accustomed to leaving the village and whose life brings them into more contact with their village neighbours than does their husbands' work.

The Dafad valley has a special place in the culture and literary history of Wales, which increases the pride of the inhabitants in belonging there. It is also well known to other Welshmen outside its boundaries. When in the 'twenties it was one of several valleys which various English town councils sought to flood for a reservoir, there was a storm of opposition and the Bill introduced in Parliament was withdrawn. Several well-known Welsh poets are associated with the valley and, like other villagers and the people of other valleys in Wales, the villagers of Pentrediwaith are very conscious of their history. They talk especially of their poets and the village hall is a memorial to them and other village worthies (*enwogion*). To be born, or even to live, in the Dafad valley is a matter of pride. Nevertheless, this pride of birth and attachment to their homes often comes into violent conflict with considerations born out of the external economic situation in which the villagers now find themselves. This was well illustrated in the controversy surrounding the plan to flood the upper reaches of the valley, for there were those, even within the valley itself, who welcomed the scheme. The nature of this controversy itself anticipates my later analysis, for in this case, as in the disputes I observed, the main public protagonists were 'outsiders'.

One Member of Parliament made this point in the Commons debate, when he alleged that the only support for the scheme in the valley came from two stranger publicans. On the other hand, the leader and organizer of the opposition to the Bill was also not a native of the valley. At this distance of time, it is difficult to get a clear picture of what the inhabitants themselves thought, but I have no doubt that the village was far from unanimous on either side and that the outsider-protagonists were in fact champions of two opposing village factions. A local newspaper's report of a Council Meeting held in the village at about the same period is headed: 'The Water Scheme Collapse—A Council Chairman's Regret'. It reads:

At a meeting of Castell Rural District Council at Pentrediwaith on Tuesday, the Clerk formally reported that the Water Bill had been withdrawn and that the beautiful valley would not now be submerged.

1st Councillor: 'That is a very good job.'
The Chairman: 'I think it is a bad job.'
2nd Councillor: 'Is there any possibility of the Bill being revived in the near future?'
The Chairman: 'I think that it is a bad job for the valley that the Bill has not been carried through. It would have brought wealth to the valley and water to the inhabitants.'
3rd Councillor: 'And have helped to relieve unemployment.'
1st Councillor: 'And made our housing problem more acute.'

Rees, in a discussion on why the Llanfihangel farmer stays in Llanfihangel, despite economic difficulties, quotes the fatalistic proverb: 'A chick reared in Hell will want to remain in Hell'. In Pentre the situation is not accepted with resignation. It is a live issue. In conversation and behaviour the more alert villagers exhibit an uneasy equilibrium of indecision. They debate with themselves and with one another whether to stay and endure a daily journey to work of ever increasing length, or to leave, once and for all, and seek their fortune elsewhere.

Another factor binding villagers to Pentrediwaith is the Welsh language. Not only does the cultural complex of Pentrediwaith make villagers feel strangers elsewhere, but it also provides a weapon against encroachment from outside. Even before the present critical state of the village economy came about, the Welsh language had a special importance. This arose out of the complexities of the development of economic classes in the course of Welsh history. For as we have seen, landlords and quarry-owners were not only rich but also English-speaking. Opposition to them forged a national patriot-

ism among the Welsh villagers and gave to the language a
greater importance than as a mere vehicle of communication.
This is, of course, true of all languages, but Welsh provides a
special case. The Welsh language is to many Welsh people a
symbol of their national identity, and they are determined to
preserve it against English encroachment. Welsh has an
emotional value for many of those who speak it, analogous to
that of Hebrew for Zionists. The position of the Welsh language
in Pentrediwaith today is therefore symptomatic of its transi-
tional position in Welsh society.

It is generally believed in neighbouring towns that Pentrediwaith is entirely Welsh-speaking, and villagers themselves
assert that this is so.[1] The truth, however, is more complex. In
Glyndafad at the head of the valley Welsh is the universal
language, and the farmers who comprise most of its population
have a different attitude to the language from that held in
Pentrediwaith. The difference is epitomized by an anecdote
told me by a former conductor of the market bus which went
each Wednesday from Glyndafad by way of Pentrediwaith to
Bigtown. He is a villager, born and bred, of a Welsh-speaking
father and an English-speaking mother. Pentre villagers
travelling on the bus usually addressed him in English, as they
did in the village, and he became accustomed to working in
English on the bus. Consequently if he was addressed in Welsh,
he usually replied in English. This was accepted by villagers
but not by those from Glyndafad, who on more than one
occasion refused to pay their fare or to leave the bus until they
had been properly answered in correct Welsh.

The only Welsh-speaking person in Pentre who would
knowingly speak Welsh in my presence was from another part
of North Wales. For, much as many villagers resent having to
speak English, it is considered extremely rude to speak Welsh
in the presence of someone who does not understand it, or even
before a villager with an English-speaking mother. One
woman, a school teacher, who spoke (and taught) very good
Welsh and was born in the village, was never addressed or
even answered in Welsh, because of her English-speaking
mother. In the house where we lived we shared a kitchen with

[1] In *The Place of Welsh and English in the Schools of Wales* the percentage of
Welsh-speaking children in Pentre schools is given as 40-60.

our hosts. They used to change to English when we entered the kitchen, and back to Welsh when we left, whether the subject of the conversation concerned us or not, and sometimes in the middle of a sentence. On one occasion, when I entered a shop where a violent dispute was in progress in Welsh, the language was immediately changed to English, although the argument continued for some time before either protagonist gave any other sign of noticing my presence.

This attitude means that, even if there is only one member of a committee who is monoglot English, the proceedings of the committee are held in English. The Women's Institute is the traditional women's organization associated with the Church and English, but in Pentre even the rival British Legion (women's section) works in English. When a notice appeared in the village advertising a meeting of the *Sefydliad y Merched* in Glyndafad, people told me on enquiry that it was some women's organization but they did not know what. I discovered only from the dictionary that this was the Welsh name for the Women's Institute. Similarly, amongst the men's social groups the Football Club and the British Legion (in its very rare meetings) discussed their business in English. The Young Farmers' Club, which is the Dafad Valley Branch, and the Young People's Society of the Baptist Chapel conducted their affairs in Welsh.

The strongholds of the Welsh language in Pentrediwaith are the parish council, which conducts its own meetings entirely in Welsh, and the Chapels. At the annual general meeting and other public meetings called by the parish council the proceedings are either entirely in English or bilingual. The parish council's minutes are kept in Welsh and read in Welsh at the annual meeting. But even this practice was questioned in 1954. After the minutes had, as usual, been read in Welsh, and summarized in English for the benefit of those unable to understand Welsh, a Welsh-speaking council member said he thought the minutes should be read in English. He said: 'We are all educated enough to understand English, I hope.' The chairman replied that it was in the regulations that the minutes be kept in Welsh, but the councillor put the resolution: 'That the minutes be kept in Welsh but the main facts be made known in English.' And he supported this by saying: 'The English pay rates and are entitled to hear the minutes.' This was seconded, with great diffidence, by an English-speaking rural district councillor.

The Baptist Chapel carried on all its proceedings in Welsh; only once in 1953, when a visiting preacher was unable to speak any Welsh, was a service held in English. The Wesleyan Methodists did in 1952 hold monthly services in English, but these came to an end in 1953 when their English lay-preacher became vicar's churchwarden to the Anglican church. English-speaking Nonconformists are forced therefore to attend Church if they live permanently in Pentrediwaith and wish to attend any service at all. The Church of England in Wales in Pentrediwaith has both Welsh and English services, but the latter are more popular even among Welsh-speaking members of the congregation. It is one thing to speak informal Welsh at home or in the shops, and another to follow the Prayer Book service and sermons in academic Welsh.

The presence of English people in the village, and the villagers' politeness about language, weakens the position of Welsh in public life, but it is by no means dead. There was a broadcast from the village hall on the Welsh Home Service during the year. Welsh plays were given, by outsiders, in the village. An attempt to cast a Welsh play with villagers failed for want of players able and willing to learn Welsh parts. Nevertheless a concert (*Noson Lawen*), conducted entirely in Welsh, was held. Welsh seemed to me to be losing ground in private more than it was in public. There are many mixed marriages, Welsh-English, some amongst the leaders of the village. Many people who speak Welsh in their homes write their letters in English and read English books and newspapers. The County Library Welsh section is little used. Pentre villagers value Welsh as a possession: they are flattered, or rather consider it natural, that English people should want to learn it, but rather resentful at their success. At the same time, many have a half-suppressed feeling that English is more 'educated', and they fully recognize the economic importance of learning to read and write good English. To participate fully in village life ability to speak Welsh is an advantage, but not to know it is by no means a grievous handicap. English-speaking villagers show little desire to learn Welsh, formally or informally, and attempts made to start Welsh classes in both 1952 and 1953 failed.

Even if someone does overcome the handicap of English birth or an English mother and learn the language, villagers do not speak to them in it. Welsh is used as a weapon of exclusion, and it is two-edged. For an incomer not to learn it is regarded as arrogant. If he tries, he is regarded as presumptuous and seeking to obtain by trickery what was denied to him by birth.

If their attitude to the use of Welsh by outsiders is clear, villagers are ambivalent in their attitude to their own use of it. It is at once a precious possession, the key to their literary and musical culture, and a barrier cutting them off from the rest of Britain. Like arguments which have raged in the village in the past over the relative merits of Eisteddfod winners and university science graduates, their attitude to Welsh reflects in cultural terms their economic and political position on the borders of Wales and England, and of the country and the town.

THE PEOPLE IN THE VILLAGE

The Dafad valley does not carry a major through road and the only traffic that comes along it from Castell brings visitors to the valley. Except in high summer week-ends, when tourists from North-Western England pass through Pentrediwaith on holidays or day trips, villagers can recognize all the cars they see. Strange ones are the subject of remark and speculation.

Five or six buses a day leave the village for Trefawr, which they reach by way of Castell. These carry men to work in Trefawr and the children to the Grammar School there. Workers and shoppers bound for Bigtown, Tonmawr or even farther afield can get other buses or trains at Castell. In 1953 the local garage started a daily service of three or four buses to Bigtown nearly sixteen miles away by their route. Two of these go as far as Glyndafad. On Wednesdays (Bigtown market day) and Saturdays there is a more frequent service. On Sunday one bus leaves at mid-day for Tonmawr to enable villagers to visit patients in the hospital there. It returns at the end of visiting time.

Although the distances covered by these buses are very

small, those villagers who are forced to use them to get to their daily work find it a real hardship. The lack of frequent services, and the fact that they almost cease entirely when there is heavy snow in winter, gives villagers (and visitors) a very strong sense of isolation and remoteness, as if they were actually living on an island. This feeling is heightened by the fact that food and provisions have to be fetched in from Bigtown. On Mondays the food shops in Pentrediwaith are either closed or have very little stock until it has been fetched from Bigtown. At Bank Holiday time one has to do enough shopping on Thursday to last until the following Wednesday, as the fresh-food shopkeepers sell out early on Friday, are closed on Sunday and Monday, and need Tuesday to replenish their stocks from Bigtown. Certain foods can only be had on certain days; fish is available only on Tuesdays, unless there is any left over next day, and meat is not available until Wednesday. Prices of meat, fish and vegetables in Pentre are usually a penny or twopence more per pound than in Bigtown. Bigtown prices are in turn a penny or twopence more than the prices quoted by the *Liverpool Daily Post* as current in Liverpool.

Most farmers and shopkeepers have cars or vans which enable them to leave the village at will, and other men may have push-bikes or motorcycles. The women are for the most part dependent on the infrequent bus services, and rarely leave Pentre. They may go regularly to Bigtown on market day, and to Chester once a year for Christmas presents or other large purchases. In the summer trips to the coast, to the Shrewsbury Floral Fete, or even to Liverpool theatres are popular. Generally speaking, however, the women of Pentre live and work in the village and have little occasion or opportunity to leave it.

The road to Castell is actually a new one by village standards, and is known as *ffordd newydd* (new road). Even the old road to Castell is only just over a hundred years old. Until the quarries became very active in the nineteenth century no road to Castell was necessary, and the main links of Pentrediwaith to the outside world were to Trefawr and to Bigtown. The road over the mountain from Trefawr is a very ancient one which joined a chapel of ease at Pentre with its mother church in the next valley. The road is impassable to all but

the most reckless motorists. It rises to above 1,250 ft. and has in
parts a gradient of 1 in 3¼. It continues as the village high
street through the village and across the river to become the
highway to Bigtown, which is possible for motor vehicles
although buses and heavy lorries prefer the other route.

Pentrediwaith is exceptional amongst Welsh upland parishes
in having its population settled in nucleated units. The largest
of these is the village of Pentrediwaith itself with about 600
inhabitants, but the hamlet of Melin, which lies partly within
the parish, also houses about 200. The rest of the parish population of just under 1,000 live in the clusters of houses on the road
between Pentrediwaith and Melin and on the farmsteads of
the estate. These outlying parts, although not far off, have a
social life of their own, and I confine myself in this book to the
social life of the village of Pentrediwaith, or Pentre.

The oldest part of the village is the original agricultural
settlement. A group of small rural-style cottages cluster near
the church. There has been a church on the hillside beside
this road since the fourteenth century. There are three terraces
of houses following the contour of the hill. One building is an
old inn, empty and ramshackle, and half of the other fourteen
are falling to ruins. Others are week-end or permanent resi-
dences for outsiders from Liverpool and elsewhere, and four
remain inhabited by older villagers.

The road from Trefawr goes down Church Hill and runs
into the main street of the village. This was built up mainly
between 1840 and 1890 to house the increasing population
brought in by the slate industry. The oldest houses are of stone,
like those of other quarrying villages, but many have now been
rebuilt in brick. The main street crosses over the Castell-
Glyndafad road, on its way to Bigtown, and houses line all
the branches of the cross-roads for a short distance. In this
part of the village are the four chapels—Scots Baptist, Baptist and, at a little distance up the valley, Calvinistic Methodist
and Wesleyan. On the main street are three public houses and
the village hall together with all the shops. There are four
main grocers, including a branch of the local Co-operative
Society, a draper, two cobblers, two butchers (one combined
with a greengrocer), a greengrocer and fishmonger combined, a baker, an electrician, two newsagents, tobacconists,

and confectioners, a chemist and a number of other small shops that defy precise classification.

As can be seen, it is in this part of the village that most of the *formal* social activity takes place. It is not, however, where most of the villagers live. There are nearly 200 people (men, women and children) living in the streets I have so far described, 150 of them in the village street itself. Of these 200 only about 25 are children under sixteen (about 12½ per cent.).[1] This is an indication of the number of retired people, widows and widowers living alone in this area.

About 300 people with nearly 70 children (about 24 per cent.) live in 92 households on the housing estate. This is situated in the angle between the Trefawr and Castell roads. In the older houses on the estate live many of the women leaders of village life and their families, several of which originated from the settlement near the church. The post-war houses on the estate are occupied by married couples with growing families, the children from which are still attending the village council school. There are still thirteen people on the village housing committee's list for council houses, and most married villagers have lived since their marriage in at least two different houses in the village or nearby. A few young married couples have houses on the council estate in Pentrenesaf but continue to be active in the social life of Pentrediwaith where their older relatives and their brothers and sisters live. During my stay in Pentrediwaith there were two cases of council tenants changing houses because of quarrels with neighbours; two other households moved out of the village; one moved to a tied mine cottage at Castell; two others changed their council houses for others at Castell nearer their work but still within the Rural District. Apart from the informal ties of neighbours and common membership of associations, there is considerable inter-relationship among nearly all the villagers on the housing estate.

The people who live actually in the village itself or on the housing estate are not, however, the only ones who take part in village social life. There are also such people as the villagers

---

[1] These figures are based on material collected over six months mainly by calling at houses and counting, but sometimes by other means. I have therefore preferred to give the figures to the nearest five.

already mentioned living in Pentrenesaf, and others in Melin and other hamlets. There are also the farmers of the parish and some on its borders who have close kin in the village, employ village lads as labourers, and come in daily to the public houses or shops. They periodically bring their families in to social events like dances, dramatic performances or concerts. Whist drives and important Chapel events draw visitors from Glyndafad and farther afield. The annual sheep-dog trials and the sheep sales bring visitors from all over North Wales and even more distant places. The local farmers seldom take office on committees as their hours of work make it inconvenient for them, and there is a little friction between them and villagers. They do, however, help in other ways by lending fields and equipment or hiring these at reduced rates, and by giving donations.

Thus two farmers and brothers, Jack and James, live on adjacent farms on the borders of the parish. James employs a man from the housing estate as a resident labourer. His sister's daughter is married to a local small tradesman who lives also on the estate. One of his sons plays for the football team and both he and his brother are keen supporters and give annual donations. His wife has brothers and sisters. One of her brothers is married to James's sister. She has a sister's daughter living on the housing estate whom she visits. James's wife attends Church with another of her sisters who also lives on the housing estate, and they go together to a Church sewing-group where they mix with other village women. The children of James and Jack, all over fifteen, spend their evenings in the billiard-room or around the place in fine weather with the other village youths and girls. James and Jack and James's wife's brothers collect in the village pub with other farmers almost every evening and both gossip and talk shop. Only some miners and farmers can afford to go to the pubs every evening; the others with one or two exceptions go only on Fridays and Saturdays. I usually spent evenings not otherwise taken up gossiping in the pub, and I was often teased about it: 'Any one would think you were a farmer, the time you spend in here!'

Another farmer lent fields for village events. He had two brothers, tradesmen in the village, and employed two village lads from the housing estate. A fourth was a noted Eisteddfod

D

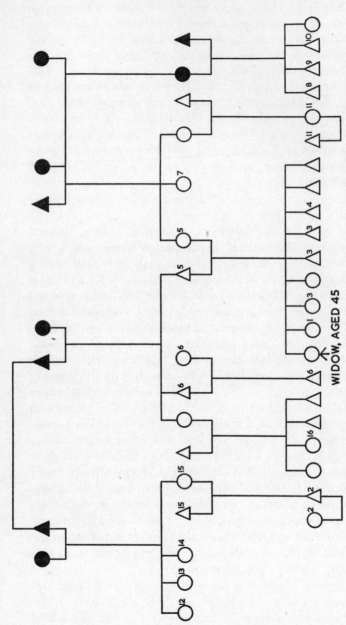

WIDOW, AGED 45

Diagram I. One example of inter-relationships on the housing estate. I have plotted the adult kin of a widow aged 45 (indicated by the arrow) on a simplified genealogy. She herself lives on the estate with a young daughter; those of her kin who live in the village or on or near the estate are numbered by households; those living outside the village are left numberless; those who have died are blocked in. I could construct similar diagrams for at least one spouse in each household on the estate. I discovered only one couple neither of whom had any relatives in the village.

In this and subsequent diagrams the sexes are denoted thus: △, male; ○, female.

performer and was friendly with several village men with whom he drank. He too employed a boy from the housing estate. His mother lived in a sort of dower house near his farm. Her father's brother's son's son lived on the housing estate, and through him and his brothers she was related to many people in the village. All the four farmers I have mentioned were Welsh-speaking and Chapel, two of them Scots Baptists in origin and two Baptists. Neither of the Baptists attended Chapel, however, although the father of one and the brother of the other had both been deacons. The Scots Baptists had followed their wives to the Church, although they rarely attended and their children went to the council and not the 'national' school.[1]

A category of villagers who do not live on the housing estate are tradesmen or the children of tradesmen, who are slightly more prosperous than the general run. Many of these own their own houses on the borders of the village. Seth is an example. He lives just outside the village. He is a builder and employs five or six of the village men. He is a Rural District Councillor, a Justice of the Peace and a devout Baptist. One of his sons, a former footballer for the village team, is now established by his father on a smallholding outside the village. His other sons are single and work for him at home. His daughter is married and lives on the housing estate. Another daughter is a nurse living away from Wales but unofficially engaged to a village boy. His wife's sisters, Edith and May, also live in their own house on the other side of the village. They are daughters of a former coal merchant and cousins to James, the farmer already mentioned. May was on the Coronation committee and plays a leading part in Chapel life. Her husband is a wage-earner employed as a driver by the owners of the granite quarry. Two of their father's brother's sons and two of his daughters live in the village, and through their father's brother they are related to at least seven households on the housing estate.

Another married couple, Jane and Tom, living on the out-skirts are both related to these sisters. Jane is their father's brother's son's daughter, and Tom is their mother's brother's son and at one time inherited and ran their father's business.

---

[1] The National (or Controlled) school is a Church foundation. These children, to add to the confusion, attended the Baptist Sunday school.

He is now a builder on a small scale. His cousin has just bought a farm near the village. Jane also has three sisters in the village, two of them living on the housing estate. Her father's sister is married and lives on the housing estate and has a family of nine grown children, all living in Pentre. She is also related through her great-grandfather with at least four other households on the housing estate.

There are other such households around the village and in neighbouring parishes, but I have cited enough to make my point. Those I have mentioned are all Baptists and Welsh-speaking and they are related, albeit distantly, to each other and to other villagers. They are all 'Pentre people' in the widest sense of the phrase, although there are other important divisions within the group that I shall discuss later. They—the people of the housing estate and the farmers I have mentioned and those living on the outskirts—are mainly Welsh-speaking, or at least Welsh-born. Before the collapse of the village economy they all earned their livelihood within the village or very near it, whether as shopkeepers, farmers, or wage-earners. The most important criterion of all, that despite their internal divisions enables them to be described as a community, is that they are united by complex informal ties which cut across and complicate their relationships on formal occasions. They are also united by ties of kinship and affinity. These ties unite the three categories of Pentre people—the people of the housing estate, the local farmers, and the house owners—amongst themselves and with each other.

Outside this nucleus, which I shall refer to as 'Pentre people', and usually outside the village as well, are a category I shall call 'outsiders'. 'Pentre people' as a category is almost but not quite congruent with 'villagers', for despite the criteria of kinship, Chapel membership and Welshness, many people are regarded by the villagers as 'one of us' who may not satisfy one or more of these criteria. The 90 people on the housing estate (30 per cent.) who profess to be Church are not thereby excluded from village membership, but in some circumstances they act in opposition to the rest.

The individuals who make up the group of real 'outsiders' were in former times landowners and quarry owners. The parish was then basically divided into economic classes. In

1955 these 'outsiders' were small traders and retired or active professional men, usually English-speaking and often church-going. The patrons and vice-presidents of Pentre societies and the judges at Pentre events come mainly from this group. Their incomes are or were derived from outside the valley and are greater than those of most villagers. Their relationships with villagers are all (or nearly all) formal and they are not usually related as kin to villagers. They cannot, as villagers do, drop in unheralded for a cup of tea or a gossip, and they are addressed formally and treated with polite respect. There are many such people in houses and bungalows around Pentre who are completely unknown to the majority of villagers. They remain nameless English visitors to all but the shops and the Post Office. There are others, however, who, although they live outside the village, are not excluded from its formal social life. They are pressed into service as vice-presidents, judges and financial supporters of events and organizations. Some-times they are made chairmen of *Eisteddfodau*, drama perfor-mances or concerts.

Thus the President of the Garden Produce Association and honorary Director of the Sheep-Dog Society until his death in 1953 was the former squire. The President of the Pentredi-waith Football Club in 1952-53 was a local publican,[1] and on his resignation, in circumstances to be related below, he was succeeded by an English immigrant shopkeeper. The 'Carnival Queen' was crowned by the foreign wife of this same shop-keeper, and the Carnival presided over by a landowner from Bigtown who owns land in the parish. The President of Pentre-nesaf Garden Produce Association was another local land-owner, who is also President of Pentrediwaith British Legion. Of these six persons only one, the publican, was normally Welsh-speaking, and all were professed Anglicans. The Bigtown landowner was the only one with kinship links to villagers; he is a cousin of the James, Jack, Edith and May already mentioned. They are on calling terms (he is the landlord of James and Jack), but he does not drop in; he calls and is treated

---

[1] There is an affinity between football and beer. The brewers are ap-proached for donations and give them, and many clubs (not Pentrediwaith) have their programmes printed at brewers' expense as a brewers' advertise-ment.

with some formality. He speaks no Welsh. All six are wealthy in comparison with most villagers.

The football club had seven vice-presidents and twelve named large-scale subscribers. Combining the two lists and allowing for the overlap, thirteen individuals and two brewery companies were involved. Of the thirteen only three spoke Welsh, and only two had relatives in the village. Twelve of the thirteen were Anglicans and one was a Roman Catholic.[1]

The list of the thirteen subscribers to the Garden Produce Association (which includes four vice-presidents) overlaps the football club list to some extent, but there are significant omissions. There are no publicans and only the Welsh-speaking shopkeeper (who is also a landowner and county councillor) appears. The breweries are also missing. Additions are the Bigtown landowner, a distinguished university professor who lives in the valley,[2] a bank manager, and two more retired gentry. Of the thirteen three were Welsh-speaking, eleven were Church, one was an atheist and one (the bank manager) Calvinistic Methodist. Only two had relatives in the village.

The Carnival fund received fifteen listed donations, two of these from other Pentre societies and one from a brewery. Nine were from local gentry, active or retired, one from the farmer Jack, and one from a local tradesman who lives on the housing estate. The remaining donation was given by an ordinary Welsh-speaking Baptist villager, but it was given anonymously. Of the eleven individuals, excluding this last one, only one spoke Welsh and none attended Chapel. Two had relatives in the village. Most (but not all) of the individuals involved had been in the village or near it for at least ten years.

All the examples I have given so far have been of individuals qualified by their income, and usually by their detachment and social status, to fill the roles of vice-presidents or recognized subscribers. There are always anonymous subscribers who would be considered presumptuous if they were to give openly. (The football club received £9 in anonymous dona-

---

[1] In more professional detail: two publicans, three retired gentry, two shopkeepers, a doctor, an Army officer, a vicar, a farmer, an official of a nationalized public corporation, and the wife of a former quarry-owner.

[2] The professor was also approached to subscribe and become a vice-president of the football club, but his conscientious objections to organized sport prevented him from complying.

tions.) On another occasion, the judging of the Coronation fancy dress, other criteria were more important than income. Strangeness was at a premium and income of little importance. It was necessary to find someone removed from kinship, or even less defined social ties, with any competitor. Two women judges of less than a year's residence were chosen—my wife and a newly established Lancashire immigrant. In the event these precautions proved superfluous, as there were so many prizes and so few entrants for the competition, postponed again and again because of rain, that every competitor got the first prize for something. One was the most original, one the most humorous, one the prettiest, etc. The prizes for most of the Coronation festivities were presented by a Lancashire business man who lived on a local farm. He was unpopular in the village and widely held to be Roman Catholic. For a similar event at the Carnival judging was entrusted to a doctor and his wife who happened to be spending a short holiday in the village.

It is important for the understanding of Pentre to grasp the part played by strangers in this community. 'Strangers' in one situation are not necessarily strangers in another. The size of the village and other factors I have already discussed make it rare for villagers who meet in pursuit of a particular activity to know each other only through that activity. Their attitudes towards each other and to attempts to assert leadership are conditioned by happenings outside the particular situation in which they are effective. The judging of the Carnival and Coronation fancy dress were not the only occasions when strangers of one sort or another were in demand. But they did not always have to be as completely strange as they were for these situations. In different social contexts different categories of strangers were employed.

The complete 'outsiders' already discussed were one source of 'strangers'. There were, however, some activities in which outsiders could not participate because of their class status. There is one particular group of non-villagers whose professional activities bring them to the village and whose services are widely used by the villagers in both official and unofficial capacities. This group includes the masters of both the Church and Council schools, the doctor, the chemist, ministers of religion, the bank manager and the assistant teachers. Some of these do have kin in the village and most are Welsh-speaking, but they are a little removed from ordinary villagers. Villagers have an ambivalent attitude towards these people; the villagers recognize their necessity but resent their alleged tendency to run things.[1] In theory Pentrediwaith produces enough of its own intellectuals to run its own affairs entirely, but in practice its own graduates do not return to live in the village. In 1953 and 1954 three villagers obtained university degrees and two others were attending universities. None of these intended to return to the village; those I asked said they would not accept posts there if they were offered them. At least two villagers hold senior teaching posts outside the valley, another is a Baptist minister in South Wales, and a fourth is a well-known preacher, broadcaster and writer. None of them comes to the village except on very short visits.

Nevertheless, the group of intellectuals, especially the teachers, do take a very active part in village affairs, and the accusation (or boast) that it is the strangers who run the village is most usually aimed at them. There are, however, others regarded as strangers in specific situations. The 'outsiders', including the intellectuals, are strangers in nearly all contexts. Even among Pentre people themselves the house-owners on the village outskirts and the farmers are sufficiently remote in most situations to be used as strangers. Finally, in nearly every group activity it is possible to recognize someone who has only that activity in common with the other members of the group or is a deviant in some respect from the distinguishing criteria of the group mainly concerned. Such a person, as I shall show, is to some extent removed from the conflicts and social pressures of full members of the group. This makes him or her of central importance in the precipitation and resolution of such conflicts.

We can summarize the community life of Pentrediwaith by saying that it is the daily social interaction of a number of individuals living in an area which centres on the actual village. The two main groups involved are 'Pentre people' and 'outsiders', but these categories both overlap and are sub-divided.

[1] See Kuper, L., *Living in Towns*. His quotation from a Coventrian on p. 37 might have been heard in Pentre. He refers to migrants: 'They try to get on committees and councils and run the town, though I suppose that type is useful.'

The division between Pentre people and outsiders was in 1953 most noticeable in a social aspect. Members of the two categories mixed informally within their own category, but on formal occasions only with members of the other. The division was also to some extent cultural; the outsiders were mainly English-speaking and most Pentre people know some Welsh even if they do not use it. Thirdly, the division was religious; Pentre people, as we have seen, include a majority of Nonconformists and the outsiders were mainly Church or nothing. In Pentre and, I believe, elsewhere in Wales, to be 'nothing' is to be 'Church'. There is a well-known Welsh anecdote, repeated by Huw Evans in *The Gorse Glen* ('Cwm Eithin'), in which a drunkard who has been expelled from all the available Chapels joins the Church. But he is too much even for them, and he is expelled from the Church as well. His mother comments that he has now missed even the last train to heaven. The story illustrates the different attitudes of Church and Chapel which I discuss below. When I was collecting systematic material, my question, 'What religion are you?' was sometimes met with a pause, followed by: 'Church'; and sometimes even answered: 'Nothing, really. But you'd better put "Church", hadn't you?'

Finally, the most significant criterion in the development of the division between outsiders and Pentre people has been economic. The Pentre people are wage-earners or small tradesmen; the outsiders are salaried, landlords, or engaged in business on a larger scale. Although I have already indicated some divisions *within* the categories, it has been necessary in general to treat them as homogeneous. Neither of them in fact is so; not only are there individual deviants within both, but they also have marked internal cleavages which cut across each other. I am not in this book concerned with the outsiders except in so far as they take part in Pentre society, and for this reason I shall not elaborate their internal divisions. From now on I am mainly concerned with the internal divisions, but external cohesion, of Pentre people.

COMMUNITY AND THE PEOPLE

Within the apparently homogeneous group of Pentre people, as I have already suggested, there are individuals who are moving or trying to move outside, and strangers who have come in by marriage or through their jobs and are seeking full recognition by the villagers. The villagers judge each other and strangers by the social groups to which they can ascribe them, and the formal groupings alone of a small village in our society are so complex that not even siblings of the same sex retain their identical social position for very long.

In Pentrediwaith social classification of each individual is not an academic exercise but is carried out in various social contexts. Its ostensible purpose is to find out if a person, X, under discussion 'belongs'; that is, to answer the question: 'Is he one of us?' 'He's a stranger really', or 'He's not really a Pentre person', are commonly heard expressions in Pentre. Their converse also arises. A newly appointed headmaster in another village is claimed as a Pentre person although he has not been in the village for many years and has no relatives left there. When I was surveying from door to door on the housing estate, after I had introduced myself and said I was studying Pentre, I often got the response: 'Of course, I am not a Pentre person myself.' Sometimes as an objective observer I could accept this, but more than once I found subsequently that the speaker had lived in the village for twenty or thirty years, or had even been born there. I have already discussed the criteria that distinguish 'Pentre people' but, as I have said, they are not absolute criteria. A 'stranger' in one context is 'one of us' in another. To list the characteristics of the 'perfect' villager is only the first stage in understanding the role of social groups within the village.

In some cases it is enough to live in Wales to be 'one of us'. In different contexts this narrows down to North Wales and to the village itself. When there was a broadcast about the village it was argued that only those born in the village were really entitled to speak. To be 'one of us' in some circumstances, membership of a particular family or Chapel is crucial. But despite these divisions villagers are anxious to give the impression of unity. They have a strong sense of community and kinship. It is a proud boast of the whole Dafad valley that 'if you tread on a dog's tail in Castell, it barks in Glyndafad'; or, as one villager put it to me, 'If you punch my wife on the nose, the whole village will come running.' In this context aspiring villagers born elsewhere will grumble that you dare not say anything about anybody in the village as 'they' all seem to be related. There is, of course, as I have already demonstrated, a good deal of truth in these assertions. But the significance of kinship does not often extend beyond its use as a tool of the villagers in their efforts to exclude outsiders. It is used particularly against those who, villagers think, bring an economic or cultural threat to the interests of Pentre people.

The Baptist minister gave a lecture on villagers' antecedents, as recorded in the registers of the Baptist Chapel, which roused great interest and discussion amongst his congregation. His tracing of some genealogies back seven to eight generations and the cross-linkages he demonstrated were, it is true, a matter of pride to villagers. But this specific pride of ancestry does not normally play a vital role in village life. In questioning villagers about their relatives, I enquired in detail for their own brothers and sisters, their father's and mother's brothers and sisters, and their children, and was usually answered in detail. I then asked for any further kin in the village. Villagers who had in fact many relatives in the village would make some comment like 'hundreds'. A great deal of pressing was required to make them specify beyond the first cousins already named. On the other hand, villagers claimed distant relatives as kin if they were distinguished or admired in some way. They sometimes denied or left out even first cousins considered disreputable. Thus the relatives of a newly appointed headmaster, or an Eisteddfod winner, claimed kinship on very tenuous grounds. But the first cousins to the mother of an illegitimate child or to someone convicted of theft will not be anxious to remind anyone of the fact themselves, if they cannot avoid being reminded of it by others. In times of misfortune, illness or fire very distant kinsmen come to each other's aid.

People are, to some extent at least, fixed in society through their connections with overlapping groups of kindred and by the direct patrineal line to which they belong. Through the latter (usually) they also owe allegiance to a particular Chapel. But outside the elementary family an individual has sufficient kindred to allow accommodation for shifts in the esteem in which he is held. If he offends the community or a section of it, some will connect him with one group of kin, some with another.

Genealogical accuracy and precise statements or relationships beyond first cousins might cause a breakdown of the whole system, and hence of the cohesive and exclusive nature of the society. People are also reluctant to list their kin lest by leaving someone out they cause a quarrel. Listing kin also involves revealing illegitimate births, and although the existence and precise origin of these is widely, if not universally, known in the village, families do not like to be reminded of them. When it was first known that I was interested in kinship links and was going to make enquiries, I was subjected to many jocular remarks about what I should discover in this house or that. In polite, as opposed to malicious or mildly malicious conversation, illegitimacy is not mentioned directly. An illegitimate person is said to be a son or daughter, nephew or niece, of a certain house or farm. The direct relationship has to be guessed, or learned by enquiry in other circles. No one ever confessed directly to their own or their children's illegitimacy. On the rare occasions when I was not able to deduce this from other material, I learned of it from village gossip.

An interesting feature of Pentrediwaith was what appeared to be a complete lack of first-cousin marriages, although villagers questioned were unconscious of any formal bar or barrier. Even marriage of distant *known* cousins is rare although it does occur. Married couples I knew who were indirectly linked through previous marriages between the same families were careful to describe their exact relationships to me lest I should think they really had been related. It seemed to me that there was an internal and an external reason which worked together to discourage first-cousin marriage.

Externally, marriages, especially in Ireland and rural Wales but also, as we shall see, in Pentrediwaith, have a 'political' function in extending the range of friendship and potential aid, and in helping outsiders to become more acceptable to villagers. First-cousin marriage would restrict this.

Internally, sibling solidarity, in the parent generation, is much greater in a village, and especially, I believe, in a Welsh village, than elsewhere in our society. Consequently the relationships between the children of siblings are like internal family relations in their intimacy. Indeed, in some ways the relations of first cousins are even more 'brotherly' than those between siblings, for they do not undergo the strain of common residence in the same household, and they lack the ambivalence introduced by conflict over succession and inheritance. Thus when I made specific enquiries in Pentre about incest and other sexual or marital relations between relatives, I was given examples of fathers and daughters, and of brothers and sisters, together with tales of men who had gone abroad to marry their wives' sisters. All this was, of course, considered abnormal but not unduly alarming or amusing. When I asked about marriage between first cousins the very idea was greeted with great amusement.

In Pentre, unlike rural mid-Wales, boys and girls mix quite freely at dances and in the billiard-room. Often a couple seen out alone together even once are linked in village gossip. Before long rumour has them courting, engaged and halfway to marriage. First cousins of different sexes can go around together without raising any such comment. For them even to think of courtship or marriage would be, in the words of a Pentre acquaintance, 'a bit of a nine days wonder'.[1]

As we have seen, then, kinship in a broad sense of remote affinal and blood links is important in the village, and socially distant kin are in some circumstances treated as neighbours and friends. The belief that everyone is related to everyone else helps to maintain the exclusiveness of Pentre as a community and its unity against the outside world. At the same time, were villagers to analyse the precise nature of their interrelationships in all situations, they would reveal their disunity to the outside world. Kinship acts as a mechanism of exclusion as well as of inclusion, and an incoming stranger who can claim kinship ties is more readily acceptable; but to marry into the village does not lead to automatic acceptance, as the division of sexes within Pentrediwaith means that a husband is not necessarily brought into daily informal contact with his affinal kin beyond his wife's siblings. The same considerations apply to an incoming wife, although she has the advantage of shopping and the more vigorous social activity of the women.

In addition to the 'one big happy family' ideology which Pentre presents to the world outside, kinship or rather family

[1] See the works of Curle, Williams and Pitt-Rivers cited in the Bibliography for discussion of this topic.

(*teulu*) plays a more specific role within the village. In Pentrediwaith family seems to play a greater part in the social
evaluation of the individual than in equivalent English villages,
and it is certainly of much greater importance than in urban
areas. All sorts of characteristics, good and bad, are said to
run in families. The Joneses are said to be wild and dishonest
or promiscuous. The prowess of Hughes at a particular
branch of singing or woodwork is linked with that of his father's
sister or mother's brother. Individual bad behaviour is mitigated by reference to madness in a previous generation or made
the more heinous by being the first blemish on a 'good' family.
This negative kind of instance is cited as much as the positive.
'I was in Mrs. —'s house today and her so dirty. Such a clean
family she comes from, too.'

This kind of comment is probably well known in all parts of
our society where four or more generations of the same family
can be observed, but in Pentre it is carried farther, and where-
ever possible an individual's behaviour and opinions are
judged by these standards. In one discussion I had in Pentre
the bad behaviour in school of a certain boy was related to madness in his mother's family traced back to his great-grandfather.
The fact that he was the child of a broken home and in very poor
circumstances, I discovered only later and in another context.

When I attended the county meeting of the Parish Councils'
Association, I noticed this particularly in the informal discussions among the Pentre parish councillors at the meeting.
Speeches by delegates from other areas of the county were
considered only after the delegates themselves had been discussed at length. Each contributed what he knew of each
delegate's family and social life, and especially any past connection or family ties with Pentre people. Only when the delegate had been socially 'fixed' were the merits of what he had
said discussed.

Villagers are not generally demonstrative of affection in
public, and brothers and sisters take little special notice of
each other when they meet by chance. Even close kin reunited
after long separation do not embrace in public. They are greeted
with the same phrase, 'Welcome Home', which casual visitors
receive on their second visit. Nevertheless there are strong
feelings of family loyalty and solidarity. This is demonstrated

by co-operation over household tasks, by the honour and respect accorded to aged parents and kinsfolk, and by the long distances which members of a family will travel to be home at the Christmas gathering. Emigrants travel great distances also to visit their parents and brothers, and members of a family may gather from all over Britain to attend a funeral. In the traditional Welsh farm house there is, as Rees has described,[1] an oak dresser in the best kitchen. This is often another symbol of the *teulu* (family). It is loaded with ornamental crockery, often willow pattern, each article of which has a long family history. It also often bears family portraits and nineteenth-century samplers. Dressers of this kind are found also in the farms about Pentre, but even the best rooms of council houses have treasured pieces of china and photographs of grandparents and absent sons or daughters, brothers or sisters.

Despite the unity of the family within the home against misfortune and in opposition to strangers, in Pentrediwaith the elementary family does not always act as a social unit in its participation in village life. This is in sharp contrast to the situation described by Rees and to my own superficial observations elsewhere in rural Wales. In fact in this respect, as I have already suggested, Pentrediwaith approximates more closely to other industrial areas than to the traditional pattern for Wales.

For outside the union of man and woman in the home, and except for a brief period of courtship and early marriage, there seem to be two villages, one of men and one of women, which rarely mingle. Each has its own sphere of activity and they meet only occasionally even in youth. When they do meet, as we shall see, they often come into conflict. Both Council and Church schools are mixed, but the children separate themselves into girls' and boys' play groups. The local Grammar School in Trefawr is co-educational and classes are mixed. The daily ten-mile journey to and from it is made on a double-decker bus which serves to carry all the pupils of the valley. Boys travel only upstairs and girls downstairs. I have travelled on the single-decker bus which serves the same purpose for Trefawr Grammar School pupils who live in the villages between Trefawr and Castell. On this the boys sit at the back and the girls at the front.

[1] Rees, pp. 44-46.

In the billiard-room of the Institute, and in the café on the
road to Castell where the young unmarried boys and girls from
about fourteen upwards gather each evening, they remain in
distinct groups. At the billiard-room girls rarely play billiards
or snooker, but sit on the benches round the walls while the
boys play on the four tables in the centre. The girls sit in twos
and threes, often in conversation with groups of boys who are
waiting or have completed their turn on the tables. Older
youths tour the public houses on Friday and Saturday in
groups, or go off together to spend the evening in Bigtown.
Women and girls, with very rare exceptions, do not go to the
public houses in Pentre, although I am told that they do go
secretly in Bigtown, and elsewhere away from home.

During courtship young couples are to a great extent cut
off from their own age and sex groups. On evenings when they
are not together they are left to their own resources. After
marriage the man may go to the pub once or twice a week, but
if he does, it is almost invariably without his wife. In summer
the men work in their gardens and talk to their neighbours.
Sometimes, particularly on Saturday evenings and Sunday
mornings, groups of men collect at the Cross or the bridge just
outside the village, and talk. I am told that one or two years
ago the young men used to collect at the bridge to sing on
summer evenings. The women go to sewing classes and Chapel
functions or to the Women's Institute and the women's section
of the British Legion.

The British Legion has two sections, men and women, which
meet together only once a year at a Christmas party. Men and
women football supporters are organized in separate committees. The one for women, the supporters' club, organizes
social events and collects money; the other, the football club,
consists of men only, chooses the team and spends what the
supporters have collected. Husbands and wives make occasional
visits to friends and neighbours together for light meals or to
play cards.

The women form the most compact and the most integrated
of the two sex-groups. They, unlike the men, share the same
work problems, and spend all, or nearly all, their time in the
village itself. They meet each other in the shops, drop in on each
other during the daytime for cups of tea in one another's

houses. They discuss village affairs while sewing and preparing equipment for social functions. When in the few mixed committees there is a clash of opinion it tends to divide the committee along sex lines and the women, who have discussed the issue in advance, often win. This is discussed in detail later in my analysis of the Carnival controversy.

The Coronation Committee consisted of the parish council plus the bank manager, the schoolmaster, and a Lancashire business man, and a number of women nominated by the Legion, Women's Institute and the Chapels. At first the committee decided to hold tea for the whole village on Coronation Day. But the women engaged on other preparations discussed this and did not like it; an emergency meeting was called and the project was abandoned. In the words of the official report in the local newspaper, providing tea for all 'would mean a great deal of work and would not give the ladies much leisure. After a discussion it was proposed to confine the tea to the children and pensioners.' Later the ladies of the housing estate arranged their own celebration tea independently of the committee.

The women of the mixed Garden Produce Association Committee attended only one of its meetings. This was said to be because the male secretary would not notify them separately of the committee meetings but told one to tell the others. The meeting they did attend was called at their behest two days before the annual show, and its only action was to cancel the show.

Such social functions as dances, concerts, lectures and plays are attended usually only by the women, with a few older men. Most of the other men present on such occasions are committee members or outsiders. This is even true of dances, where women are to be seen dancing together. It is a remarkable sight, after a concert, to see the crowd of men packed on the narrow pavement opposite the entrance to the village hall, waiting to take their wives home. Even whist drives during the year are sparsely attended by men and 'ladies' have to play as 'gentlemen'. For this they receive a bonus of points and therefore often win. This situation is reversed at Christmas time, when the men attend to get their hand in for the British Legion's annual 'Feathered Whist' at which the prizes are all

E

poultry. The weekly so-called house-to-house whist drives held
in private houses in aid of various village funds usually attracted
between sixteen and 'twenty players. Just before Christmas
as many men as women come to these. For most of the season,
however, one of the school teachers and myself were the only
men to go.[1]

In all societies there is a division of sex roles within and outside the elementary family. But as we have seen in societies
such as that of the Irish peasantry described by Arensberg and
Kimball, this very division forges the family into an organic
unit because of the complementary nature of the male and
female roles. In Pentre, however, although this survives to a
slight extent, the process has extended outside the elementary
family and created a real division which is felt and resented
by Pentre people. The women's organizations flourish while
the men's British Legion and football club struggle, and the
brass band and male voice choir have capsized altogether.
Villagers attribute this to the fact that men have to go away to
work and the daily journey leaves them too tired to organize
their own recreations when they return.

Pentre is not alone in this situation. The second world war
and its aftermath brought what is almost a second industrial
revolution to Wales. Kenneth Harris has an illustration from
the South in one of his articles on Wales which he wrote on his
return from America. It is impressive, even allowing for
journalistic exaggeration. It appeared in the *Liverpool Daily
Post* on 3 August, 1953:

> Yet even though half a million Welshmen left Wales
> between the two World Wars, Welsh culture seemed to hold
> its ground. The Choir, the Chapel, and even the coalmine—
> where on Mondays, deep in the black bowels of the pit,
> miners discussed the sermon as they swung their picks—were
> its repositories.
>
> Then the strange paradox began to be revealed; the
> prosperity of the two-and-a-half million who live in Wales
> today seems to corrode the nation's life as poverty never did.
>
> I heard the best account of it in the kitchen of an old tin-
> plate worker a mile or two from Llanelly. [In South Wales]...

[1] The larger whist drives in the village hall attract 80-120 players, both
men and women, some of whom come from Glyndafad, Pentrenesaf and
farther afield.

'Now take Rhys Watkins who used to live next door,' he
said. 'He used to work in the tin-plate works over in the
Cym. He was a craftsman, used to work by hand. He knew
all the other men in the works—they were his butties—because
it was small, and he knew everybody here in the village,
because that's small too, you see.

'When he came home from work, he used to go up to the
Chapel two nights a week—choir on Thursdays—all Welsh
hymns and anthems you know—and chapel meetings on
Fridays—electing a new deacon, or wondering how to pay
for the new organ or something like that—and all in Welsh,
you understand. Of course, Rhys was out of work as often
as he was in. But he had roots, roots that went back to the
old Wales.

'Now look at Rhys Watkins. Rhys isn't here any more.
They've shut down that little tin-plate works, you see. Not
economical—too small, too far from the road, and too old
to put this new machinery in. So Rhys had to go and work
in Port Talbot—big mass producing plant, thousands in it.
He just looks after a machine.

'When he got home, he was spending two hours a day in
the bus mind you, he was too tired to go and sing and he
lost interest in the chapel. Good pay, mind you, oh yes,
I'm not saying. Last month Rhys moved to the new housing
estate they've built in Port Talbot, quite near where he
works. Lovely place, too—bathroom, electric fire, everything. But no chapel, no choir, not even a pub. So there's
Rhys bach—money in his pocket but no roots. Television
but no oratorio. And all Wales is gradually going where
Rhys is now.'

This is the state of affairs which inspires the Welsh Nationalists to demand self government for Wales.

This state of affairs, or a movement towards it, in Pentrediwaith also inspired the women to grumble. In discussion on this
article when it appeared, and in later discussions on the same
theme which followed the Welsh Home Service broadcast from
Pentre, there were hotly opposing views. One of the older men,
himself independent of the need to work for wages, a prosperous tradesman, painted an idyllic picture during the course
of this broadcast of his youth in Pentre. Many of the women
agreed with him, and recalled the nightly Chapel activities of
their youth. The older working men could remember the un-

employment, and although they resent the long journey to
work prefer to have adequate money in their pocket. They do
not regret the old days which they remember for their hardship, not their culture. The younger men do not have the same
attachment to the village, and resent the daily journey less.
Some villagers suggest that because they can get only poorly
paid and unskilled jobs they are left frustrated and uncaring.

It appears to me that the collapse of the village economy
does account for the men's apathy, but in a different way.
Their enforced daily co-operation with non-villagers has
turned their attention away from the village to the amusements and problems of the world outside. The young men regard the village as somewhere to sleep and eat, but they go to
Bigtown and Tonmawr not only to work but also to amuse
themselves. One of the football club's biggest difficulties was
to get jobs done after Saturday home matches. The young men
on the committee and the village players wanted to catch the
evening bus to Bigtown. Similarly, the bus carrying Pentrediwaith to play away from home often had to travel through
Tonmawr, and on these occasions more of the passengers got
off there to watch Tonmawr's professional Third Division
team than accompanied the team the rest of the way to its own
match.

Even though the men are apathetic in the carrying on of
their own organizations, they are vigilant against the encroachment of women on to their own preserves. They both resent
such attempts and act against them. In this they are aided by
the other women. No sympathy is expressed for a woman working or managing a business without the help of a man, and
her difficulties are magnified and ridiculed. 'Lady doctors'
are mistrusted. Women who turn up to public meetings on
political affairs which are not considered to concern them are
shamed by public and sarcastic reference to their presence.
The opening 'Lady and Gentlemen' always produces a laugh
from the men and a blush from the lady. On one occasion
several women told me they were going to attend a meeting and
have their say. In the event only one came, and she sat silent
at the back. When I enquired the next day the reason for the
absences, I was told: 'Several of us looked in, but we wouldn't
have felt comfortable with all those men.' (There were about

seven or eight men present.) When a visiting brass band brought a woman instrumentalist with them, all the local speakers made jocular reference to her and she looked very uncomfortable. Pentre women rarely enter pubs and when they do all the men fall silent and stare. It takes considerable courage even for an outsider to withstand this treatment.

RELIGION AND SOCIAL CLASS

In this section I am not trying to give a comprehensive picture of the place of religion in the life of Pentrediwaith. I am only concerned with religious groups in their specific role of extending the range of kinship and creating new formal and informal social ties. Chapels, like football clubs and sheepdog societies, pursue their own specific ends, but in a society where social differentiation is important they cannot help influencing, and being influenced by, divisions within the society. It is from this point of view that I describe them. The dogmatic differences in the beliefs and practices of the Nonconformist sects are not significant in the internal organization of the village.

Outside both family and the vague group of kindred to which an individual belongs is the organization of the village into religious groups and its extension outside the village to the chapel circuit and beyond. There are, in or near Pentrediwaith, a church of the Church of England in Wales, and four chapels. All these draw their congregations from the village only in part; one or two draw most of their members from outside the village.

The two chapels actually in the village itself are the small Scots Baptist and the large Baptist chapel. The latter is referred to by villagers as 'Capel Mawr', the large chapel, and is the only one of the four village chapels which had its own paid resident minister in 1953. Pentre is known in North Wales as a Baptist village and the Baptist chapel claims some 300 members. I was unable to get precise figures of membership from this chapel, but I have seen congregations of at least 150 attend on important occasions. Of 212 professed Chapel members on the housing estate 178 were Baptists, 15 Scots Baptists, 13 Calvinistic Methodists, and six Wesleyan Methodists. (These figures include children.) In the rest of the village of 188 people 117 were professed Chapel members, 68 pro-

fessed Anglicans, and three Roman Catholics; 91 of the 117
Chapel people were professed Baptists, 24 were Calvinistic
Methodists and two were Wesleyan Methodists.

Alwyn Rees has described for Llanfihangel how each Nonconformist sect has its own Sunday schools, its own hymns and
its own heroes. He tells how the child growing up into a chapel
receives a section of his education in common with his chapel
fellows, and in distinction from that of the children of other
chapels. He has pointed out also that this may even extend to
a knowledge of world geography, as a child learns most about
the country where the denominational missionaries do their
main work. It is possible, bearing this in mind, to regard the
chapels of Wales not so much as religious organizations
expressing a particular theological point of view, but as social
groupings of extended kinship. For while the theological
reasons for schism are no longer remembered by chapel-goers,
the social rift between the chapels remains and invades every
sphere of social activity. An individual is expected to, and
usually does, favour his kinsmen against non-kinsmen and his
fellow members against members of other chapels or the Church.

Thus in Pentrediwaith there are three grocers' shops and the
Co-operative Stores. They are served by the same wholesalers
and manufacturers and their stock is very similar. Two of these
private shops were kept by Baptists until recently and one by a
Methodist.[1] Generally speaking, villagers shop according to
their religious affiliations. The Co-operative Stores are patronized mainly by Church members and Wesleyans. Even when
the shops cease to be owned by Welsh Baptists and are
bought by English incomers they are still preferred by many
Baptists to the Welsh but Methodist stores.

Most social functions are held in aid of some charity; and
while all are supported on a reciprocal basis by members of
different sects Timothy, who did not attend a function in his
own Chapel and then went to a concert in aid of another
Chapel in a different village, was attacked quite strongly for it.
The Baptist Chapel, in particular, and the other Chapels
on a smaller scale, run a weekly Sunday school for all ages and

[1] In Pentre, and as far as I am aware elsewhere in Wales, Calvinistic
Methodists are referred to as Methodists, and Wesleyan Methodists as
Wesleyans. I adopt this terminology.

a 'Young Peoples' Society' on a week night in the winter.
The latter holds concerts, quizzes, lectures and play-readings
as well as an annual party. Both the 'Society' and the Sunday
school run by the Baptists are attended by people of other
denominations, but the committee members are all Baptists.
Immigrants to the village who belong to other denominations
not represented tend to go to the dominant Baptist Chapel.
The school staff and the bank clerk mentioned provide examples of this. Despite this admission of outsiders young Baptists have more opportunity to meet their Chapel fellows, and
courtship between them wins the approval of the adults more
readily. The Chapels are therefore largely, but not entirely,
endogamous.

Although members of different Chapels may attend different
Sunday schools, they have a day school in common. Most
Church children attend the National school. Again, as its name
implies, the Church of England *in* Wales is regarded as an
importation, whereas the Chapels, entirely Welsh, are not.
Chapels sometimes, as at the Coronation, hold services in
common; but a common service of the Church and Chapels
together is very rare indeed. An Armistice Day service was
the only one I observed. The distinction between Chapels
arises only in specific contexts, but the division between Church
and Chapel is more fundamental though even this latter is
bridged by informal ties at the village level.

The historical development of this division is well known.
In the nineteenth century the Church was associated with the
landed gentry and the Chapels with their tenants. There was
a bitter struggle by the Chapels to be recognized, and to bring
about the disestablishment of the Church. The scars of this
struggle still remain in Pentrediwaith as symptoms of the
cleavage in the community between outsiders and Pentre
people. In fact, the Chapels were also introduced from outside,
and it was not the poor farm labourer who made the initial
break with the Church but the small tradesmen and the yeo-
man farmer:

> The hell-instructed grocer
> Has a temple made of tin
> And the ruin of good innkeepers
> Is loudly urged therein.

The historian of the Diocese of St. Asaph puts it more formally than G. K. Chesterton:

There are also other elements of a more mixed and doubtful character, such as the profitable turn they give to their principle of brotherhood (*teulu y ffydd*) in its social bearings; for they are much more exclusive in their dealings than Churchmen, and make it more a point of duty to promote the interests of their own members; hence a shop kept by a dissenter will often thrive, which if kept by a Churchman would fail of support; and it generally happens that the shopkeeper is a leading officer in the Chapel.[1]

In Pentre in 1953 two of the four Baptist deacons were shop-keepers but the general mass of villagers had adopted the Chapel as their own. They used it in their conflicts with outsiders.

Today the Chuch has services in Welsh and ordinary villagers *do* belong to it. Church functions are patronized reciprocally by Chapel folk, and Chapel members join the Church dramatic society. Nevertheless, an underlying hostility remains and occasionally comes out into the open. The rift is most marked in Pentrediwaith between the Baptists and the Church, and least between the Church and Wesleyan Methodists; and it is not a mere historical survival, for the very pattern of Nonconformist religion intensifies and prolongs it. Yet, as we shall see, it is not an absolute division. Family and other ties may cut across it. Sunday school outings provide an example. In 1954 Baptists, Methodists and Church all went together. This was because the Church was then without a Vicar; and it provides another illustration that the gap between Church and Chapel can be bridged. In 1953, however, there were separate trips for Church and Baptist. I was fortunate enough to be invited to join both of these. The similarities and differences between the Baptist-organized and the Church-organized outings well illustrate the differences in attitude and social behaviour between Church and Chapel.

Although the Chapel trip was organized by the Baptists, ostensibly for Sunday School attenders, many others took part. It is an annual event and in 1953 the party went as is usual to a North Wales coast resort. Three packed coaches hired from the local garage took us there in the morning and brought us

[1] Thomas, D. R., *History of Diocese of St. Asaph*, 1874, p. 150.

back in the evening. Inside the coaches the emphasis was on the family. Each father (when he was able to come) and mother and their children of all ages sat together in the coaches from start to finish. We were affiliated to the family in whose house we lived. It was an extension of Sunday behaviour as it should be, of the family taking part together in Chapel life (an ideal seldom realized). Social relations between families and friends were the same before, during, and after the trip. When we had arrived at the coast, the coach loads split up into their family groups and each family went its own way according to its own inclinations. We all met together again at an appointed time in the evening and rejoined the buses. On the way home once more families sat together. The younger children slept, the adolescents were kept under close surveillance, wearing their best clothes and on their best behaviour. If wagonettes had been substituted for charabancs the Victorian atmosphere of the occasion would only have been slightly enhanced.

The Church outing was in complete contrast. Only the Vicar in charge of the party and ourselves were over eighteen years old, and there was only one coach. We stayed together as one group all day and toured places of interest in North Wales. Only at the place where we spent forty-five minutes for lunch and at a coast resort where we stayed two-and-a-half hours before going home did the party break up into groups. There was a minimum of surveillance and the maximum of 'pop' drinking and high spirits. At the beginning of the day the boys sat at the back of the bus accompanied by two of the 'wilder' girls, and the girls sat in front. The Vicar sat right in front and kept his eyes straight ahead. My wife and I were at the pivotal point of this internal arrangement. On the way home only the Vicar and ourselves remained in our original places. The division of the sexes, which was slightly modified after every halt both going and returning, had disappeared almost entirely. Boys and girls sat in couples. We stopped on the way for a final purchase of 'pop' and chips in newspaper. Not only were the type of outing and the behaviour on it entirely different from the Baptist trip, but the composition of the group was very different. Several of the travellers could speak no Welsh, and they were drawn, in the main, from two classes. Some were children of comparatively wealthy outsiders living in or near the village. Others were children of poorer villagers, or lapsed Chapel members.

These two outings show the differences in Chapel and Church organization very clearly. The Chapel is an association of the respectable and the virtuous, people who belong to the community and who belong, through ties of kinship and intermarriage, to each other. A fall from grace (such as having an illegitimate child) is a fall from Chapel. But the Church remains open to the fallen. The Church combines two social functions: it provides religious organization for the outsider and it gives a social position and religious education, if not to the 'fallen' themselves, who rarely seek it, at least to their children. The Church, then, in Pentrediwaith at least, caters for the 'outsider' in all senses, while the Chapel is for the saved, for those who 'belong'.

There is one other religious category that needs brief mention. Pentre people expect all their fellow-villagers, and anyone else with whom they come into contact, to belong to some religious body. Those who do not claim any Chapel membership they usually ascribe to the Church. Sometimes, however, someone with no apparent allegiance is thought to be Roman Catholic. There are very few Roman Catholics in Pentrediwaith, but the practising ones are well known as they go to Mass in Castell by taxi early on Sunday mornings. Villagers, especially Baptists, are very hostile to Catholics. The Minister preached more than once in 1953 on the twin evils of Catholicism and Communism, in that order. When the Catholics announced that they planned to set up a 'Mass Centre' at Pentrediwaith, the meaning of the word 'Mass' was misunderstood and caused misapprehension and fear amongst villagers.

When the choice of judges for fancy dress competitions was being discussed one person who was otherwise in every way suitable was rejected on the ostensible grounds that she 'was not used to that sort of thing'; but it was explained to me afterwards that the real reason was that she was a Catholic. Finally, a business man, who had bought a farm in the neighbourhood, and who had become for various reasons very unpopular with villagers, was noticed not to attend Church. It was assumed that he must therefore be Roman Catholic.

The split between Church and Chapel is not as absolute as it was in the past. As we have seen, many ordinary villagers are members of the Church. Church and Chapel villagers combine in a common allegiance to things Welsh. There is another annual bus trip from the village which goes, at least when it is within a day's journey there and back, to the Royal National Eisteddfod of Wales.[1] Every second year when the 'National' is held in North Wales the village entertains a brass band from South Wales which comes to compete in the National Eisteddfod and gives a concert in Pentre the Sunday before. The 1953 concert gave rise to a chain of circumstances which are discussed in another context below (p. 125). Pentre people compete in the 'National' from time to time and a winner of the 'blue riband' for the best performance by a vocal soloist lives in the village.

When a question of nationality arises the division into English and Welsh may, and does, cut across Church-Chapel boundaries. Elfed, the blind preacher and hymn writer, who was Minister of King's Cross Welsh Congregational Chapel, was not the less admired by Baptists and Methodists although he was a Congregationalist. When Sir Herbert Dunnico, a famous Baptist preacher, who although born in Wales had worked all his life in English Baptist congregations, died in 1953 few in the village had heard of him, although he was sufficiently eminent to earn a column of obituary in *The Times*.

[1] Care must be taken not to confuse the Royal National Eisteddfod of Wales (*Eisteddfod Genedlaethol Frenhinol Cymru*) known as the 'National' with the parvenu International Eisteddfod at Llangollen. The 'National' is an annual event held in alternate years in North and South Wales. The central events are the crowning and chairing of the bards who have been adjudged best in literary competitions in Welsh. There are also competitions for choirs, solo voices, a form of singing called 'Penillion', and other musical performances. The proceedings are conducted entirely in Welsh, and directed by the Gorsedd of Bards of the Isle of Britain led by the Archdruid. Most of the competitors are drawn from Wales itself, and those who do come from outside have to perform in Welsh. It has been held continuously for at least eighty years and claims a tradition of three or four centuries.

The International Eisteddfod at Llangollen is a sort of Junior Edinburgh Festival, with folk dance and folk singing contests combined. Competitors come from all over Britain and Europe, and sometimes farther afield, but they perform in their own language or style. Although the International has Welsh characteristics and draws its inspiration from the National, it is not a national festival in the sense that the latter is. The Llangollen event has been established only since the last war.

Although, generally speaking, people remain in the denominations to which they are born this is not always the case. Husband or wife in a mixed marriage may abandon his or her own Chapel for that of the spouse. Internal quarrels are said to cause people to change their Chapel allegiance although I know of no cases of this from personal experiences. I know of two cases of divorced Churchmen from the neighbourhood of Pentrediwaith remarrying in Chapels outside Pentre. As we have seen, Welsh-speaking incomers drift towards the Baptists and English-speaking incomers to the Church. The English-speaking Vicar's Churchwarden in 1953 had been lay preacher of the Wesleyan Methodists in 1952.

When I was told by a villager, 'If you punch my wife on the nose, the whole village will come running', I took it to mean, as I was intended to, that the whole village were her kin. But there are other reasons why she might get the support of some villagers and not others. Proximity, sex, close family, broad kinship, religious affiliation, and Welshness are all ties which unite villagers with each other. But not all villagers are united by all these ties. Each sees himself as the centre of a group of kindred and friends who will come to his aid, or who have other obligations towards him and claims on him. No two villagers are the centre of the same group and the groups surrounding each overlap and intermesh. This is a major factor in giving the village its cohesion. The very characteristics that unite some divide others within the group of Pentre people.

Between Pentre people and outsiders there are, as I have shown, fewer ties and more divisions. Informal ties, especially of kinship, are reduced to a minimum. But the two groups are linked in other ways which both unite them into one society and determine their respective roles within it. Pentre people try to bring outsiders into social activity to solve some of their problems of decision and organization. Outsiders allow themselves to be so used because of their desire to conform with expected patterns of behaviour associated in the English past with the squire and his tenants. Thus village society in this stage of its history goes some, if not all, of the way towards uniting in a community of interests those who on the national level may be bitterly divided.

III

POLITICS AND THE COMMUNITY

COMMITTEES AND LOCAL GOVERNMENT

IN the last chapter I described how society in Pentrediwaith includes not only 'Pentre people' but also 'outsiders'. Members of both grouped categories belong to other groups and are linked to each other by various ties. No individual villager belongs to exactly the same groups as any other villager. I shall now proceed to the analysis of the division and cohesion of groups of villagers in specific situations. The first of these is the formal interaction of Pentre people and outsiders in the local government organization of this area.

As I have suggested, even within the group of Pentre people there are deep conflicts underlying the appearance of unity that they present to the casual visitor. In the organization of committees Pentre people employ devices in order to avoid thrusting the responsibility for open schism upon themselves. This responsibility is forced upon either outsiders or other 'strangers'. Strangers, however, do not form in any sense a corporate group. A stranger in one context is not, necessarily, a stranger in another. In order to risk unpopularity in a limited sphere of activity it is not necessary to be an outsider to the whole village, but only to be remote from those groupings whose immediate interests are affected or whose feelings are hurt.

Bound up with this question of the taking of unpopular decisions is the more general problem of leadership. For while Pentre people are prepared, in some circumstances, to accept the decisions of outsiders as binding upon them, they are sensitive to any attempt at uppishness on the part of fellow people of Pentre. Amongst themselves they consider that one man is as good as the next. This was made clear to me in a discussion on the failure of the local brass band. The band

65

failed even though it had an expensive set of instruments and an adequate number of skilled players. Although there are two experienced conductors in the village, the band does not play since it is felt that an outside conductor would have to come in to conduct rehearsals twice a week. This would cost two pounds a week and his fares, so that the band would run at a loss. When I asked why they could not use one or both of the local conductors, it was explained to me just what one of the band would say (and had said in the past) if he was told to do something by one of his 'mates'.[1] At football matches and other social events quarrels often arose through one person's allegedly trying to boss another. The same problem in another form arose in the football team, the captain of which, a young villager, could never be persuaded to give orders, on or off the field, to the players. In previous seasons this problem had been solved by having an outside captain, a West Indian Negro from a nearby town.

In all social activities in Pentrediwaith and in all the committees set up to carry them out this authority problem arises. Committees must have a chairman, choirs and Eisteddfod parties a leader. This leader must somehow contrive that the organization not only achieves its aims, but that it does so without at the same time splitting itself or village opinion. Ordinary villagers do not relish or seek this role, which is usually thrust upon someone who is at least a stranger, if not actually an outsider to the village. But the position of chairman, or leader, is not the only one allotted to the stranger. For in those committees which, as a member, I observed most closely, however deep the division of opinion among the villagers, they held back their views until a stranger was forced by the course of the discussion, or by specific request of the chairman, to move the motion which revealed the split in the committee and allowed discussion of it to come completely into the open.

These considerations apply in particular to the internal organization of the village. There are, during the course of a year, numerous social events and activities which village

[1] The problem in this case was not, as might be supposed, merely the difficulty of choosing which of the two local conductors to have. One of them, by age and experience and family connection, was an obvious choice.

opinion demands must be organized only by properly constituted committees. Some of these events are partially restricted to particular groups of villagers, such as members of
certain chapels or the British Legion (women's section) or the
Women's Institute. Others, like football matches or the
carnival in 1953, are felt to be the concern of the whole village.
But all committees are limited in their behaviour by the
interests and desires of Pentre people and of the slightly wider
society of which Pentre people form the nucleus.

The activities of the organs of local government differ
sharply from these as, through them, Pentre is brought into
contact and conflict with the other villages of the rural district,
with the other districts of the county, and ultimately with other
counties and the national institutions of England and Wales.[1]
Yet historically it is the relationship of the villagers to the
outside world which, as I have already suggested in a previous
chapter, colours if it does not determine their internal relations.
It is not therefore surprising to find that it is in local government that one can see most clearly the conflict of interest
between outsiders (in the special sense in which I use the term)
and the villagers of Pentrediwaith. It is in local government
also that it is most obvious that this division is an economic
one. Pentrediwaith local councils show a familiar picture of
economic class division and antagonism.

Economic classes are not mingled at random in any one
council in the local government organization of Pentrediwaith.
On the one hand the parish council is predominantly wage-
earning, and on the other the county councillors and magi-

---

[1] There are some Church and Chapel organizations which also bring
villagers into contact with external groups. But conflicts in this situation
are rarer and less spectacular and I do not feel I have sufficient first-hand
knowledge of Church and Chapel politics to do more than mention my
awareness of their existence.

On the other hand, I knew all the local government councillors personally
and had frequent informal discussions with them, and I attended five
public meetings in the village. Further, I accompanied the Parish Council
delegation to the annual conference of the County Association, for which
opportunity and many other kindnesses I am deeply indebted to the
Council and its Chairman. Finally, as the possessor of both a typewriter
and willingness to use it, I was entrusted with the task of handling much of
the correspondence of the Pentrediwaith Ratepayers Association. I betray
no trust in quoting from my experience in these respects as it was well
known that I was writing 'a book' about what I saw.

68   VILLAGE ON THE BORDER

strates are salaried or self-employed, as the following table shows:

Table I

FIGURES IN THE POLITICAL LIFE OF PENTREDIWAITH

	Salaried	Self-employed	Wage-earning	Church	Chapel	W	A
M.P. for County (1) ..	—	1	—	1	—	—	—
County Councillor for Rural District (1)	—	1	—	1	—	1	—
Rural District Councillors for Village (3)	2	1	—	2	1	1	1
Magistrates for Valley Petty Sessions (8)	2	6	—	6	2	2	—
Parish Councillors (6) ..	1	2	3	1	5	6	5

W indicates Welsh-speaking.
A indicates persons active in village life in other spheres than politics.

The differences are even more striking than they appear to be in the table when the individuals actually referred to are considered. Thus, of the three rural district councillors two live outside the village and the one Welsh-speaking Chapel member has reduced his village contacts to the minimum. At one annual meeting of the parish council this last district councillor (although not of course mentioned by name) was singled out as the least likely of the three, on past experience, to side with the villagers when the parish council and the rural district council came into conflict with each other. The salaried parish councillor is a teacher (but not in the village) and the unpaid minister of the Scots Baptist Chapel. He was chairman of the parish council for most of 1953 and for 1954. The salaried members of the other bodies are two doctors and the manager of the 'Co-op'. One of the self-employed parish councillors is actually the junior partner in a local business owned by his elder brother, the county councillor. The other is a small-scale jobbing builder who employs only one man and a boy with whom he himself works side by side. Both live in the village itself and speak Welsh. The self-employed rural district councillor is an undertaker as well as a builder, but on a larger scale than the builder on the parish council. Four of the six self-employed magistrates are large landowners.

Only one man from amongst the rural district councillors, the Bench of magistrates and the county councillor takes an active part in village life outside local government. He is the manager of the local 'Co-op' already mentioned and he is a rural district councillor. He lives on the village high street, belongs to the Church, and speaks no Welsh. His services as chairman are much in demand. Five out of the six parish councillors are otherwise involved in village life, one as a minister, and others as Chapel deacons and society secretaries.

Apart from their class composition, the activities and proceedings of the various bodies illustrate their differing class outlook. The proceedings of the Magistrates' Court, which meets in Pentrediwaith on the last Friday of every second month, show this most sharply. The infrequency of its meetings and the economic situation which, by forcing the men away to work, causes most misdemeanours that are committed by villagers to occur outside the court's jurisdiction, result in most of its cases being very minor ones. The rare cases of theft, for example, that have come up since I have known Pentre have been tried in Bigtown, where the alleged offences have taken place.

The local Petty Sessions dealt with one or two cases of poaching, licensing applications, marital disputes (*in camera*), and minor offences like failure to obtain television licences and riding cycles without lights. But even in these minor affairs the remoteness of most of the magistrates from the lives of ordinary villagers is very clear. Villagers are, of course, fully aware of this themselves and comment on it in discussion. Although some individual magistrates are popular outside the Court, when some particular case brings the proceedings of the Court to the notice of the villagers they comment unfavourably on the Court's remoteness and lack of understanding of the daily problems of 'our kind of people'. For example, in one poaching case the young defendant, after being found guilty, asked the Bench for leniency on the grounds that he had an uncertain income of only five pounds a week and his wife was expecting a baby. He was told that if he could not live on five pounds a week he had no business to marry and have children. Another occasion which was held to show the Bench's remoteness arose when the Court was trying to assess a litigant's means in connection with an application and counter-application for the variance of an illegitimate child maintenance order.

F

Some of the magistrates expressed surprise that the man involved, who lived by catching rabbits and selling them to farmers, could produce no receipts from the farmers, or any other accounts except a weekly profit or loss entered in his pocket diary. Since the average value of these transactions was only six shillings it would have been surprising if he had had these records.

Although there have been periods in the history of Wales when the Magistrates' Courts played a significant role in social life and when their class nature was important, during 1953 they played little part in the lives of the great majority of Pentre villagers. The branch of government which concerned villagers most closely and the one in which they had the most interest was the parish council.

The parish council meets about once every three weeks, in private, although in theory any member of the public can attend.[1] It conducts its proceedings entirely in Welsh. Councillors explain, when asked why they do not meet in public, that their affairs do not concern outsiders and that any villager who wants a say in its deliberations can stand for election. It has maintained its independence of the English squire and gentry by insisting on its all-Welsh rule which, of course, excludes them.

The parish council gives an annual report to the public at an annual general meeting at which the other types of councillor also report. I attended two of these meetings, which were both conducted mainly in the English language. The attendance at such meetings is usually poor in Pentrediwaith, although the desire to organize Coronation activities made 1953 a record year in this respect. This poor attendance does not signify public apathy towards the parish council and its works, for the parish councillors are themselves Pentre people and very actively engaged in village social activity. Their decisions are noted and informally discussed both in the village at large and with the councillors themselves. On important issues they cannot long remain in ignorance of village opinion. Their active position in social life makes them particularly sensitive to informal pressures, which the comparative outsiders who

[1] There is some dispute about the legal position of Parish Councils in regard to admission of the public.

become rural district and county councillors or magistrates can easily avoid. The fact that their critics in the village refuse to come into the open and voice their criticisms at the public meetings called for the purpose only makes the critics more annoying and the criticisms more effective. Nor, since parish councillors represent the voice and interests of all Pentre people, can they themselves abdicate power to outsiders and put their disagreements and worries on to strange shoulders, as do less vital committees. The parish council have partly solved their problem by retreating (as other committees also attempt to do) more and more into secret session. Pentre parish council (unlike that of neighbouring parishes) usually refrains from sending reports of its proceedings, or even its decisions, to the local newspaper. One of the chairmen who held office in 1953 told me that he used to send in reports, but they led to trouble with villagers who questioned their accuracy, so he stopped sending them.

I could not attend any of the private meetings of the parish council, so I cannot say how and with what difficulty they reach decisions. I have, however, no reason to suppose that they differ greatly from other Pentre committees. Evidence in this direction is that the three chairmen who officiated at meetings during the year were all, in some senses, strangers to the rest of the council. One lived outside the village in the hamlet of Melin, and of the other two one was a Wesleyan deacon and one the Scots Baptist Minister. It is, perhaps, significant that no member of the Baptists, dominant both in the village and on the council, was chosen for this post. It is also significant that no member of the parish council was a close relative of any other; this is in contrast, as I shall show in the next chapter, with other committees. When a husband and wife both stood for election to the parish council, the wife was rejected mainly, I think, because she was poaching on masculine preserves.[1] But the reason villagers gave for not voting for her was that her husband was already on it, and 'it isn't fair to have two from the same family'. This seems to me to confirm the parish council's representation of the whole body, and not just a section, of Pentre people.

[1] At a County Association Meeting I attended only one delegate in nearly two hundred was a woman.

The parish council's activities in 1953-54 were summarized by the chairman at the annual meeting and show how it forms the medium through which ordinary villagers put pressure on the higher councils.

(1) They tried (at the request of villagers) to get motor licences issued at Pentre Post Office, on the grounds that if they were issued at Castell, why not at Pentre? The executive of the County Association took this up.

(2) They arranged the demolition of a ruined building in the village which was considered an eyesore.

(3) With the support of other parish councils in the valley they opposed a move of the National Insurance offices.

(4) They had a footpath in the village widened.

(5) They held a public meeting about work in the valley.

(6) They negotiated (unsuccessfully) with the National Trust to let the latter's field in the village be used as a children's playground.[1]

(7) In response to a petition from the residents they had approached the Post Office to erect a new pillar box at one end of the housing estate.

(8) Through a sub-committee they collected money to buy public seats for the aged to commemorate the Coronation without charge on the rates.

(9) They had had meetings with the Rural District Council about street lights. (The chairman expressed a hope that the councillor present would take it up.)

After some other minor activities, which included negotiating bus times with the company, had been listed, the chairman of the parish council concluded by saying: 'We have done our best to keep the other councillors on their feet. One district councillor, not the one present, threw cold water over all our schemes. The parish councillors were elected to serve Pentre and so were the three rural district councillors, and they should not forget it.'

But the parish council does more than merely represent and work for the interests of Pentre people in the rural district and the county. It is not actually responsible for presenting the

[1] From correspondence I have seen, this question seems to have been under discussion for about fifteen to twenty years.

policies of the county and district to the villagers, nor for implementing decisions taken by the national Government. Villagers and councillors however behave as if it were. This gives the parish council a critical position in the administrative structure of Pentrediwaith. The parish council appears to face both ways. Thus at a meeting to set up a ratepayers' committee to deal with the problems of the schools and work in the valley (see below p. 83) a suggestion was made that the parish council be constituted the committee. The suggestion was rejected for many reasons, not all of which were made explicit, but the remarks of the Baptist minister in opposing it clearly reflected the villagers' view of the parish council's role. He suggested that the committee to be formed should consist of the officers of the council together with the elected representatives of the ratepayers. He said that the school managers, of which he was one, were in a sense only the little servants of the county administration. If the audience could see the school managers' minute book they would find it 'plastered' with recommendations that the County Council ignored. In the same way the parish council and even the District and County Councils were only servants. 'The ratepayers', he concluded, 'represent the voice of the people, and will be listened to, because they are voters.' His analysis of the duties of local government was wrong in law but represented the common view of the village.

The *Liverpool Daily Post*, in an article commenting on the meeting of a County Association of Parish Councillors,[1] gave the other, and correct legal, viewpoint. The writer said: 'Untrammelled by direct responsibility for the major services, they act as a sort of detective agency spotting the shortcomings of the "higher-ups" and prodding them to do something about them.' A contradiction in function of this kind is inherent at a particular critical point at the base of all hierarchical systems.[2] British local government is not intended to be hierarchical in this sense, but it is easily misinterpreted by those not aware of the law.

Apart from the part they play in the internal affairs of

[1] 'Day to Day in Wales', 21 September, 1953.
[2] See Barnes, Gluckman and Mitchell where this is explicitly stated. It is implicit in other sociological analyses. See, for example, Whyte, W. F., *Human Relations in the Restaurant Industry*.

villages, parish councils through their County Associations unite the common people (*gwerin*) as a class against other classes in the community, themselves organized in the Rural District Councils Association, and against the external restraints of the County Council and even Parliament. In the village situation class interests of the *gwerin* are also local interests of the neighbourhood. The outsiders who represent Pentre on the higher councils do not represent the village alone but a larger area which includes other villages with their own local interests. Thus the complications introduced by the differing class composition of different local government institutions are still further increased by the different scale on which the various councils operate.

At the same time the internal divisions in the County Association reflect the divided rural and urban, Welsh and English, interests of wage-earners in different parts of the county. The proceedings at the annual conference of the County Association of Parish Councils provided me with additional evidence that it was the urban-rural division rather than the Welsh-English division which was primary. One reason for this was the slightly anomalous position of the village of Pentreglo, which is both Welsh-speaking and industrial. The attitude of Pentreglo representatives to any issue was, as I shall demonstrate, crucial.[1]

Not all parish councils in the county belong to the County Association, and during 1952-53 there were three withdrawals and one new member. The Association has not long existed and the chairman at its annual conference in 1953 alleged that those parish councils which had not joined were those which had on them councillors who were also district and county councillors. On the other hand some members present appeared from their speeches to be themselves members of the County Rural District Councils Association.

The county is roughly divisible into its rural west and industrial east: the parallel, on the county scale, of the general division of Wales into rural north and industrial south. This division of the county, though not geographically exact,

---

[1] It is not my purpose here to describe the history and present state of parish councils in Britain. Their importance in this area of North Wales is highly exceptional.

is sufficiently near reality to make it necessary for the Parish Councils Association to meet in alternate years in the east and in the west. It will be remembered that the National Eisteddfod takes place in alternate years in North and South Wales. Thus two issues which arose at the 1953 conference underlined this east-west division in the county. They were concerned with telephone kiosks and Welsh devolution. The result of the first was compromise. One of the responsibilities of parish councils is to mediate between villagers and the Post Office Telephone Service. There was considerable discussion on the theme of whether the Post Office should be pressed to erect telephone kiosks first in industrial areas where they would be much used, or in isolated areas where, although they would be used less, they would be essential in vital crises. The conference split east-west on this and only reunited on the belief common to all village representatives that public kiosks should have priority over private houses.

The lines of cleavage revealed by this preliminary 'skirmish' were followed again in the discussion of the second and more fundamental issue of Welsh devolution. The debate was opened by the representatives of a parish in the rural west of the county who put the motion:

That this Council is strongly of the opinion that the formation of an Association of Parish Councils for Wales would be advantageous and in the best interests of rural parishes, and asks the County Association to take the necessary steps to bring this about.

The very able proposer of this motion seemed at first sight to provide an argument against my description of the class basis of North Wales parish councils, for he was a medical practitioner. In fact, however, it is a case of the 'exception testing the rule'. He was very popular with his fellow-delegates and in discussion afterwards I heard it said: 'He is not really like a doctor at all. He could easily leave the village and earn a lot in town, but he prefers to stay with his own people. He is like one of us.' The terms in which this evaluation is made, and indeed the necessity for making it at all, appear to me to confirm the usual class basis of the parish council, at least in North Wales.

To return to the discussion on devolution, the doctor's main argument was that the National Executive of the Parish Councils Association were unfamiliar with Welsh problems in particular and all rural problems in general. They were, he said, 'Sirs, admirals and lords'; in fact, not 'our kind of people' at all. He repeated this phrase in Welsh and was loudly applauded. Further, he argued, Shrewsbury would be a more convenient meeting place than London, as parish councillors were often people who could not afford time and money to go far afield to the bigger council meetings. A heated discussion followed this opening statement and it was noticeable that English accents spoke against, and Welsh accents for, the resolution. Finally, despite allegations that the resolution was the thin edge of the 'political' wedge, and that it was connected with the 'political' Parliament for Wales Campaign, and despite a summing up by the chairman which was weighted heavily against it, the resolution was carried by 33 votes to 14, with many abstentions. The division was as it had been for the telephone kiosks. The Pentreglo delegation, although they were Welsh-speaking and represented one of the traditional homes of Welsh nationalism, spoke and voted against the resolution.

This is not an isolated piece of Pentreglo behaviour. Thus in 1954, when a conference of North Wales parish councils was called in Colwyn Bay, it was announced that the conference would be conducted entirely in Welsh. In these circumstances, it was not the English-speaking parish councils of North Wales which raised an outcry but this entirely Welsh-speaking one. This parish council not only protested to the County Associations and to the press, but even went so far as to boycott the conference entirely. The people of the all-Welsh rural areas, and the people of marginal villages like Pentrediwaith, where the language of the village is, in ideal, Welsh and the language of work is English, regard the people of Pentreglo as treacherous and unreliable. Rural Welshmen see the issues involved as part of a struggle to maintain Welsh language and culture against English encroachment. The industrial areas, even if they are centred, as Pentreglo is, on a Welsh-speaking mining industry, know that they share economic interests and problems with neighbouring English-speaking towns and similar English industry. They realize, as the rural areas do not, that they cannot escape co-operation and consultation even if they wish to.

Pentrediwaith people often speak slightingly of Pentreglo and accuse its people (sometimes with justice) of trying to dominate county affairs, and especially the educational system, the churches and chapels. Pentreglo's proud boast of a teacher or preacher from every house is a source of continual irritation to aspiring intellectuals in other and smaller villages. The attitude of the Pentreglo delegation to two other resolutions at the County Association conference was pointed out to me as being 'them all over'. When it was suggested that larger parishes could ease the Association's financial burden by making a larger annual contribution, the Pentreglo delegation strongly resisted the suggestion. They suggested recruiting other parishes or raising the subscription all round. Pentreglo has a population of between ten and fifteen thousand. Yet later they themselves brought in a resolution (which they failed to carry, the matter being referred to the Executive Council for further discussion): 'That the Pentreglo Parish Council is of the opinion that the present number of delegates appointed by the larger parishes in the County to attend the Annual General Meeting of the Association should be increased'. Even to an impartial observer Pentreglo appeared to be wanting it both ways. To the representatives of villages already jealous of Pentreglo's power this was further confirmation of their perfidy.

The attitude of Pentrediwaith people to Pentreglo, whose people must be recognized as Welsh yet which represents a threat of domination similar to that of English outsiders, is paralleled by their attitude to 'South Walians' (as the inhabitants of South Wales are termed). They distrust the Nationalists and the 'Parliament for Wales Campaign' for the same reason. The threat against their group identity from advancing English industrial power has engendered an opposition to all external groups. Pentre villagers would rather stay in isolation than risk domination by either English or Welsh 'outsiders'.

The rural doctor, supporting his council's proposal, said, as I have already reported, that parish councillors were often people who could not afford time or money to go far afield. This statement provides us with the key to understanding how the social classes come to be separated out so neatly into the

different councils in semi-rural Pentrediwaith. All local government representatives are of course unpaid, although they do
receive expenses. Pentre Parish Council meets in the village,
in the evenings and only once every three weeks. The Rural
District Council meets in the daytime once a month at Bigtown
or Castell, and the County Council, also in the daytime,
quarterly at the county town. There are also committees to
attend. The wage-earner who puts up for election to these
bodies has not, it is true, to face loss of wages, but he has the
problem of finding transport to these centres. Further, district
and county councillors represent a larger area, so that those
whose occupations bring them a wider range of contacts are
likely to be elected, and these in present conditions are rarely
wage-earners.

Nevertheless, although, as I have tried to show, district
and county councillors are more remote from ordinary villagers
and their problems than are the parish councillors, their
lives can be made uncomfortable if they make unpopular
decisions. Their reaction to this is very similar to that of the
parish councils. They 'pass the buck' to their fellow-councillors
or other institutions and retreat into secrecy. Although they
are required by law to admit the public, this obligation is
easily evaded by going into committee. Few villagers are sufficiently incensed about an issue to risk making themselves unpopular by insisting on attending, even if they had the time,
the desire or the means of getting to the meetings. Councillors
may even stay away from meetings likely to make awkward
decisions. This may be the reason why only eight of the twenty-
two members attended the annual Rural District Rating
Meeting in March, 1954, which raised the Dafad Rural District
rates by one shilling and twopence.

WORK FOR THE VILLAGE

In this section I want to illustrate the role of strangers in
Pentrediwaith in respect to the political situation. Later we
shall see that, where the education of the children is concerned,
the religious schism in the village overrides its unity in taking
decisions; but Pentrediwaith in 1953 was united in the common
aim of bringing back work to the valley and securing a Modern
School. But even with interests in common there was always

danger of disunity carried over from other spheres of social activity, and at crucial points in the discussions it was left to a stranger or outsider to put the critical question or proposition.

At the same time I shall discuss some of the general characteristics of public activity in Pentrediwaith, with particular reference to the initiation of new activities. By doing this I hope to show that, although most public activity appears to be the preserve of the few, it is deeply rooted in village society. Activities which are not so rooted do not long survive. In Pentrediwaith entertainments and other recreational activities are rarely undertaken for their own sake. They usually have a public purpose. When tickets for various social functions are sold in Pentre the first questions asked by a prospective buyer are not: 'What will happen at the concert?' or 'What is the play?' but: 'Who (i.e. what society) is running it?' or 'What is it in aid of?' Thus, in Pentre theory, a dance is not organized because it is a long time since the last dance but because the football club or the Women's Institute needs funds. Whist drives, on the same theory, are held not because people want to play cards but because the British Legion has a benevolent fund to be supported or the parish council wants to celebrate the Coronation with memorial seats.

Sometimes the process is reversed; a band or choir wants to perform in the village and a charity has to be found for it to aid. Rarely, then, does one person run an entertainment or some other activity on his or her own. The public has an interest and expects to be represented by a committee. A committee should have a chairman, a secretary and a treasurer and some members. In the Pentre view this ensures that nobody 'puts anything across' the villagers. Deviations from this simple pattern lead to failure. When, in 1953, an individual did run his own band concert it started a great deal of trouble. The first reaction from many villagers was to refuse to help accommodate the bandsmen. One reaction I heard was: 'Why should I put up some old bandsman and feed him, just to line old Charlie's pocket?'

An English outsider, retired and come to live not far from the village and active in the W.V.S., tried to start an old people's club in the village during 1953 and was at first unsuccessful. Not only were the old people themselves suspicious but she had difficulty in getting usually active women villagers to help her. Activities are not so easily and informally started in Pentrediwaith.[1] Another attempt, this time to start a branch of the N.S.P.C.C. in the village, was only a little more successful although it observed the formalities. In this case the prime mover was the English-speaking wife of the Anglican Vicar. She called a public meeting in the Institute and invited, by printed invitations, between thirty and forty of the active village women of all denominations to attend. Only four or five went and two of those were outsiders, but a secretary was appointed and some small social events were organized. The aim of the branch was to collect funds to help the Society's activities elsewhere. Support was very slight. I heard several village women comment that there were no ill-treated children in Pentrediwaith and the villagers would be better occupied in sticking to matters in which they had a more direct concern. There was in fact no public demand in Pentre for a branch of the N.S.P.C.C.

The significance of the failure, or near failure, of these two attempts to initiate new activities is made clear by two that succeeded. One of these was the Carnival discussed in detail later. The other is an example in the field of political activity: the formation of a Pentrediwaith Ratepayers' Committee with the aims of (1) bringing back work to the Valley, and (2) agitating for the fulfilment of the County Council's original plan to build a Modern School in Pentrediwaith. Even this was only a partial success, as it also failed to fulfil all the necessary conditions which seem to be essential if a new activity is to succeed. The discussion of how it began and what happened to it illustrates my view that only activities which arise formally in response to informal discussion amongst Pentre people themselves have any chance of surviving. Further, like the Carnival, the project had a direct, specific and limited aim, and it tried to enlist the support not of men or women alone, or of another sectional group, but of the whole community.

The two main themes of Welsh history, for the last 50 years at least, have been the struggle by Welsh Nonconformists and

---

[1] Her attempts did finally arouse village interest and by September, 1954, the organization had been put on a more formal basis and appeared to have had some success.

others for independent education, and the problems of poverty, unemployment and under-employment.[1] It is not therefore surprising that very soon after I arrived in Pentrediwaith, and even during the first phase of my stay there, it was impressed upon me that work and education were the principal political interests of the villagers. They were considered as interrelated and were inevitable subjects of conversation amongst both men and women wherever I went. In the first few weeks of house-to-house surveying, I often had to persuade people that I was not carrying out the first stage in a government plan to restore work to the valley. Work and education were the main themes of both the annual parish meetings I attended. But the village was not united in its attitude to either. I try to show this below for education. Where work is concerned, the men over 35 press for the reopening of the quarries, but this does not attract the young men and girls who would only benefit if some more highly-paid secondary occupation were introduced. Nevertheless, village opinion was united on the main issue, namely that it would be a good thing for all if work could be provided in the village. Although the most active advocates of this are the older men and the tradesmen, no one openly or publicly works against it, or even suggests that it is undesirable; its 'opponents' merely refrain from activity on either side.

At the parish meeting of 1953 the parish council's own report carried no reference to either work or the school, although it was the council who called the subsequent special meeting on these topics. Their role in the events was characteristic. As a parish council they have no direct concern with labour administration, which is in the hands of the local Employment Exchange of the Ministry of Labour, or with education, which is the concern of the County Council. Yet as villagers and councillors they are the most liable to informal village pressure on both subjects, and in some cases they were directly threatened by approaching unemployment. They were felt in

[1] Thus Professor David Williams writes in *Modern Wales*, p. 289: 'The primary factor in the social life of both rural and industrial Wales was, therefore, the existence of acute unemployment. Throughout this period the unemployment rate for Wales was consistently far higher than for any other region in the United Kingdom'; and again, at p. 291: 'All social and political developments in Wales between the wars were conditioned by the overwhelming fact of unemployment and its consequences.'

the village to be the right persons to put pressure on the Ministry and on the County Council, and yet their impotent position prevented them from doing so. They called the meeting but were rejected as agents to carry out its decisions. The lengthy report in the local paper does not mention the parish council at all. Their unhappy middle position emerged clearly in the discussion.

The County Councillor who raised the issues at the village annual meeting had a double interest. As a village tradesman and landowner he had a direct interest in bringing work back to the village and staving off depopulation. He was not anxious for a separate committee to be formed, but he owed his election as County Councillor (or so I was told and so I deduced from his speeches) to his promise of vigorous action on both issues. In his report to the annual meeting he emphasized his own personal efforts at the County Council meetings. He said that he was leaving no stone unturned in his efforts to get work back to the valley, but that he was not on the Planning Committee of the County Council. Dafad Rural District was represented only by Castell on this committee, which seemed to be under the impression that the Dafad valley was in the neighbouring county. He quoted, without comment, a Ministry of Labour reply that there was ample work within easy reach. He was interrupted by a shout from the audience: 'That means twelve bob off my pay packet.'

Turning to the school, the County Councillor related his own efforts to get a modern school for the village and recounted the difficulties he had met with from other councillors and the permanent officials. At this 1953 annual meeting he was still on the side of the village. When the special meeting was held he had weakened, or accepted the inevitable in the valley conditions. He supported the County Council at the meeting on the movement of the infants to the Church School. By the 1954 annual meeting he was himself an active advocate of the County Council's solution.

After the 1953 annual meeting in March discussion continued in the village, but it was overshadowed by Coronation preparations, the celebrations themselves, and their aftermath. When all this had died down, printed notices appeared in the village shops reading:

Pentrediwaith

PARISH   COUNCIL

The above Council invite all Ratepayers from
the Valley to:

A PUBLIC MEETING

at the

COUNCIL SCHOOL, PENTREDIWAITH

on

July 1st 1953 at 7 p.m.

To discuss the following business

Agenda:—

(1) Employment in the Valley.
(2) New School.

The notice was not, to my knowledge, actually exhibited in
the valley outside Pentrediwaith itself. Pentrediwaith is only
one of four parishes in the valley and the audience were all,
with two exceptions including the County Councillor, not
only from within the parish of Pentrediwaith but also from
within the village itself. There were twenty-five men and an
English woman from just outside the village present at the
beginning of the meeting and thirty-four men and five women
at the end. This was (justly in my experience) considered a
good attendance by the villagers. It should not be taken as
indicating widespread indifference to the meeting. Many men
preferred to spend the evening in their gardens but nevertheless
joined in the general informal discussion which preceded and
followed the meeting itself.

The meeting, which had been called by the parish council,
was nominally conducted by its Vice-Chairman, a bus-driver
from the nearby hamlet of Melin; the original suggestion of
forming a ratepayers' committee had come from the Chairman
of the parish council, a Pentre Council roadman. But control
of the meeting was soon taken by the Baptist Minister who made
it appear as if the proposition had come from himself. He
argued in its favour that government bodies would not listen
to individuals but *would* listen to groups who represented rate-

payers. He implied that this advice had been given to him by the former M.P. for this area.

The proposal to form a committee of ratepayers was put (as usual) by a stranger. This was the manager of the local Co-operative Stores who, although Welsh-born and originally a Wesleyan, can speak little or no Welsh. He was, in 1953, Vicar's Churchwarden and a Rural District Councillor. In this case there was no division and the proposal was accepted by acclamation. Election of the committee was then proceeded to. The Chairman called for nominations. Silence. The stranger spoke first. He suggested that the parish council be the committee. The Baptist Minister immediately opposed this. The committee in his opinion should be made up of parish councillors as officers, together with elected representatives of the ratepayers. It was at this point that he made the statements, already quoted, alleging that the parish council were in some senses only 'the little servants of the County administration. . . . The ratepayers are the voice of the people and will be listened to because they are voters.'

After this statement there was a pause while the meeting temporarily left the subject of elections and proclaimed itself, by general agreement, a meeting of ratepayers. A member of the audience then asked who was on the last committee. Nobody could remember. When I made enquiries afterwards no one could remember if there was a last committee or what it could have been for, let alone who was on it! This move was standard procedure in Pentre at all the meetings I attended whenever it was necessary to elect a committee. To seek precedents in this way helps to avoid making new decisions and invidious comparisons between rival candidates.

Thus at the annual parish meeting in 1953, when a committee to run Coronation celebrations was in course of formation, this sort of discussion occupied most of the time. 'What did we do for the Jubilee?' and 'Who was on the Jubilee Committee?' were two of the questions asked. It was in fact suggested on that occasion that the parish council look up the records of the Jubilee and do the same again. In practice, although precedents are always sought for particular lines of action, written records seldom exist in Pentre to establish them. If the records do exist they are usually inaccessible, and so freedom of action in response to existing conditions or desires is maintained.

When the ratepayer's question failed to bring any response, the Chairman asked the County Councillor to say who ought to be on the committee. He declined at first to do this, saying a committee could do nothing on the work issue and that the County Council had valid objections to building the school. Discussion about forming a committee was therefore, in his opinion, futile. The Minister replied, followed by an Englishman, later a principal in the infant school controversy, who suggested that the meeting press for a factory halfway down the valley from Pentre. This suggestion was not only not supported but was also bitterly attacked as a surrender to outside powers. For although the meeting was advertised as being for the ratepayers of the valley, and bringing work 'back to the valley' was the phrase in which aspirations were expressed, it was in reality entirely a village affair. The needs of Pentrenesaf or even Melin were not of interest to it.

The Chairman once more came back to the topic of elections and after much discussion it was decided to have a committee of five. The Rural District Councillor, who had before suggested the whole parish council, now suggested the Chairman and Vice-Chairman (one, as I have said, a council roadman, the other a bus driver). The County Councillor raised sufficient interest in the committee idea to oppose these men on the grounds that committee-members would have to accompany visitors to the quarry, and perhaps visit Shrewsbury (headquarters of the quarrying company), the county town or London. It was therefore unfair to ask working-men to serve. The County Councillor himself, the Minister, and the Rural District Councillor were the only ones of those present (excluding of course myself) who were not working-men or their wives, and his objection was not taken seriously. The Vice-Chairman of the Parish Council retorted that it was an illusion to suppose that brains were confined to those who had money.

After further nominations a committee was finally chosen by declaring all those nominated to be elected. There was no voting to choose five of them. The committee consisted of the Baptist Minister, the Chairman of the Parish Council and another parish councillor, the local garage-owner, the doctor

G

(a District Councillor) who was not present at the meeting, the County Councillor, and a village building-worker. When the committee first met a week later at the Minister's house, five of these attended. They were the Minister himself, the two parish councillors, the building-worker, and the doctor. Absent were the two self-employed members of the committee—the garage-owner and the County Councillor.

The committee drafted letters on both issues, had them typed, and sent them to the County Council, Ministries, Members of Parliament and other public figures. They collected samples of stone and sent them to quarrying companies. They tried to conduct a survey in the village of what men who had formerly worked in the quarry actually did in 1953, and how far they had to travel to do it. But they had little success and became discouraged, until finally their interest and activity almost completely faded away. At the parish meeting in 1954, it was mentioned that the committee had been formed and had been active, but that was all.

Village opinion was united in support of this committee, and although there is a division between the young and middle-aged on the points at issue, English-speakers, Church-goers and even some outsiders, could and did unite with Welsh-speaking, Chapel-going villagers on the issues. The committee was defeated not by apathy within the village, as happened with the other unsuccessful projects described, but by superior forces outside the village. Against these and in isolation they were impotent. One village in Wales which excluded even the closely neighbouring villages from its aims and counsels could not hope by its unaided actions to reverse, in its own favour, processes which a whole nation cannot adequately control. When actual unemployment comes to the village of Pentrediwaith, as seems inevitable in the near future, this committee will, I have no doubt, come to life. Even then it is unlikely in isolation to influence the course of events. The class structure of local government and the relative lack of power of the parish council means that those who are most closely affected by external changes in economic and social conditions are the least able to alter the trend of events. Conversely, County Councillors and Members of Parliament, especially in rural districts, are the last to become personally aware from their own direct experience of the effect of national and county policies on the people they represent. In rural North Wales at least, this was as true of Labour and Liberal party candidates for office as it was of Conservatives.

Apart from the more general issues involved in the events I have described, they also throw light on the internal organization of social activities in Pentrediwaith. For, despite the failure of the committee to achieve its aim, its short-lived success within the village reveals the four stages which seem to me essential for the initiation of new activities in Pentrediwaith. These stages were also passed through by the Carnival during 1953. They are:

(1) Informal public discussion and agitation;

(2) The raising of the matter at a formal public meeting for 'official' discussion;

(3) The calling of a special meeting with limited and specific aims. This was achieved only because there was an existing body (the parish council) to call the meeting, and a number of villagers sufficiently interested to attend; and

(4) The emergence of a new organizational system with the sole function of carrying on the new activity.

Thus, although the meeting was called by the parish council, the final committee elected by the meeting rejected the council as a body and, with two exceptions, as individuals. The meeting was recorded in the local paper without any reference to the parish council at all. This last fact can be interpreted either in terms of a temporary unpopularity of the parish council because of the failure of the Coronation festivities, or because of the ambivalent position of the parish council as an institution. I think there is a more fundamental reason than either of these. The football and the supporters' committees suffered the same fate after their initiation of an annual carnival. Before the war the Girls' Friendly Society lost control of its offspring drama group. One committee cannot serve two masters, and once activities have been set in motion by existing organizations they develop a momentum of their own which often sweeps the originators to one side. People not interested in, or at feud with, the original committee and its aims rally to the new standard. The new committee formed in this way accepts the sole function of carrying on its new job, nor will villagers allow it to extend its own functions. It may bud off new committees in its turn, but like all parents it is seldom successful in retaining control of its mature offspring.

In the next section I analyse a situation in which the villagers were less united. Divisions amongst Pentre people bequeathed to them by their history and intruding from the wider society of Wales complicate the internal social life of the village.

EDUCATION IN POLITICS

The importance of education in the life of Wales is well known, and an account of the controversies surrounding the subject in Pentrediwaith in 1953 and in the decade 1895-1905 will illustrate one of the main cleavages in the society in both periods. This is the division into Church and Chapel. In 1895 and in 1953 there were two schools in the village of Pentrediwaith, a non-denominational Council school, and a Church school. The latter is also known as the 'National' and, since the 1944 Education Act, as the 'Controlled' school. Since, broadly speaking, those villagers who are not Church are Chapel members, the Council school is, in effect, a Nonconformist school.

According to a contemporary pamphlet, in 1894 the national education authorities ordered the Pentrediwaith School Board to remedy the fact that accommodation for infants was insufficient for the average attendance. This order was repeated the next year, with the additional warning note that, if it should not be carried out, the Board would consider either removing altogether, or substantially reducing, the school's grant. Plans of the required enlargement were prepared, forwarded by the local Board and approved by the national body. Then, apparently quite suddenly, the Pentre Board were ordered to cease operations until the school had once more been inspected. In September, 1895, the Board of Education changed their minds and said that no enlargement was required. The Board of Education ensured that no enlargement was in fact carried out by refusing to sanction the necessary loan. The Pentrediwaith School Board thereupon asked what they could do to accommodate the extra children, and they were told that the surplus could go elsewhere. The Board of Education backed this up with a threat to the School Board that they would in any case reduce the school's grant if overcrowding continued. The only possible place for the village children to go was, of course, the Church school. The Pentrediwaith School Board pointed out that ninety per cent. of the village children at that time were Nonconformists, and again sought permission to expand, citing the reports of the Inspector in support of their case.

A few years passed without further development. Then, in November 1898, the Church school was declared inefficient by the Inspectors and its managers were warned. In 1899 the Inspector's report stated that the Board school was 'a very efficiently conducted school' but that the accommodation was insufficient and that the attendance must be reduced or the accommodation increased. In 1900 the Board of Education again encouraged the school's plans for enlargement, but once again they changed their minds. They said their previous encouragement had been given in error. Now they wrote: 'The School Board must take steps to reduce the average attendance.' In 1900 there were sixty children in the infant classroom with only six square feet per scholar; by 1903 there were eighty-six in the infant class, and the Inspector said that 'the cloakrooms must not be used for teaching.'[1] In August, 1903, insufficient space had become a problem in the Church school as well, and there was an absolute deficiency in school accommodation in the village. In October there were 301 children filling 277 places; next year the Council school, which was supposed to accommodate 145 pupils, usually had 200 and once had 218. Classes were held in the open air:

> There was not room for all the children to sit at the desks and some sat on the teacher's desk or on the Master's desk.[2] Standards 3, 4, 5, 6 and 7 were so mixed up at times that it was not known to what classes children belonged.

---

[1] *Aids to Public Health*, p. 178, gives the *minimum* space requirement for schoolchildren as sixteen square feet. Although the Education Act of 1902 abolished School Boards and handed responsibility for education over to Local Education Authorities, it did not immediately come into operation in Wales. This was because all the Welsh Local Education Authorities, with one exception, refused to work the Act.

[2] The head teacher is still called the Master in North Wales; other masters are called teachers.

The Inspector said in his report for 1904:

A classroom which has accommodation for 24 is habitually overcrowded, over 40 children being usually in it. In the infants' classroom there were often 72 scholars present where there should have been only 45 (equal to 5 square feet per child!).

The Church school, which was given permission to rebuild in 1904 at the same time as the Council school was being refused permission, received this surveyor's report in 1905:

These buildings are very old and want renewing altogether. They are not at all satisfactory. Building is bad, roof is bad, drainage bad, the whole being in a very unsatisfactory state. Requires rebuilding.

No major changes had been made to this building since that report, at least up to the time I left the field in 1954.[1] The contemporary pamphlet from which I take the foregoing facts ends by alleging, on the evidence I have reproduced, that the policy of the Board of Education was: '(1) To prevent the improvement of Board School buildings and (2) to tolerate, and try to force children into, unfit denominational buildings to the danger of their health and at the sacrifice of efficiency.' It is interesting to note that in this controversy, as in 1953, although the battle was between Church and Chapel in both cases, spiritual dangers to the children are never mentioned.

I have given the contents of this pamphlet at some length because in 1953 the County Education Committee tried to introduce changes into the organization of village education which would, if they had succeeded, have moved all the village infants into the very same Church school buildings which were so roundly condemned in 1905. This move did not unite the villagers in opposition to letting their children spend their first years at school in an old building that was both dark and damp, and which lacked proper sanitation. On the contrary, it opened wider the always inherent division between Church and Chapel. Church people resented the denigration of the build-

[1] In 1904, of 23 denominational (*i.e.* Church) schools inspected by His Majesty's Inspectors in one North Wales county, 21 had major structural defects. The Board School in Pentrediwaith was rebuilt in 1905. It has since developed structural defects of its own.

ing as an attack on the Church. Chapel people regarded the Local Education Authority in the same light as the pamphlet's writer had regarded the Board of Education nearly 50 years before. In the discussion and agitation that followed Minister and Vicar, and Welsh and English, stood openly opposed. The Parish Council, albeit behind the scenes, opposed the Local Education Authority. The County Councillors, past and present, put the Authority's point of view. The leading protagonists on both sides were 'outsiders'. One was an Englishman married into the village and the other a shopkeeper from another village in the valley.

In 1953 both schools in Pentrediwaith catered for infants (5-7), juniors (7-11), and those senior pupils over 11 who had failed to get places in the local Grammar School at Trefawr, or to go to the Technical College at Tonmawr. When the County made its post-war plans it was agreed that the Dafad Valley should be treated as a unit and a Modern School built at Pentrediwaith. In the words of the County Reconstruction Committee's report in 1946, there was a strong case for the establishment of a new school for the reason that 'the valley is in many ways a self-contained unit with many differences between it and the adjacent districts in language, tradition, and environment' and that 'pupils from the top end of the valley would otherwise have to travel 17 miles or more, each way, daily.' At the same time the report envisaged the early demolition of the Controlled School buildings, condemned, as we have seen, in 1905.

By 1953, however, nothing had been done about this or the earlier plan, prevented from completion by the war, to set up a Bilateral Central School in the village for all children over eleven. The schoolmaster had come to Pentre fifteen years previously to take charge of this and was, in 1953, still waiting for it to be set up. He has since moved to a headship elsewhere in the county. In both county and local teaching opinion a Bilateral School would have two advantages. It would prevent the division of village youth into Grammar School pupils and 'the rest', and it would provide a centre for evening activities of both adults and children. Domestic science and carpentry, for example, could not be taught to the children, or practised by the adults in 1953, as there was a complete lack of facilities for either. By 1953 the County Council had abandoned both those ambitious projects as too expensive. They were talking of building two huts for woodwork and domestic science at an estimated cost of £6,000. The people of Pentre by no means accepted this decision, and the subject constantly arose in conversation and at public meetings during 1953. In the discussions I am about to describe, the abandonment was threatened of even the least of the three proposals.

During the summer of 1953, the County Director of Education visited the village and inspected the schools. As a result of this visit he convened a meeting of the local board of Managers. He asked the Baptist Minister, Chairman of the Managers, to call a meeting of parents to hear and give their opinion on certain proposals of the County Council's Education Committee. These proposals were that, during the summer holidays of 1953, some slight structural alterations should be made to the Controlled School building. In September, when the schools re-opened for the new year, all the village infants should go to the Controlled School building. All the juniors, together with those over eleven who had failed to obtain Grammar School places, were to go to the Council School building. Both schools were to be administered by the existing Master of the Council School.

The Minister agreed to call a meeting, and the children in both schools were asked to tell their parents its time and place. Both sets of news, that there was to be a parents' meeting at the school and that there was a threat to send the children to the Church school, drifted round the village on the day of the meeting itself. There was no formal written announcement, and the unknown small boy who had been dispatched by the Baptist Minister to tell the Anglican Vicar failed, for some mysterious reason, to arrive. The Vicar heard from his parishioners only the next day that the meeting had been held.

At the appointed time twenty-eight men and women collected in the school and squeezed uncomfortably into the tiny desks. Later, after the discussion and voting, I realized that the audience was divided, not only in opinion, but in spatial arrangement in the schoolroom. Chapel people filled the front seats, and the Church people sat in a single line of desks across the back of the room. The Baptist Minister presided and called the meeting to order. The County Council's proposals were then put by a former County Councillor. He was a magistrate and a shopkeeper in the nearby village of Pentrenesaf. He had been invited to the meeting by the sitting County Councillor who had defeated him in the last election. One of the main issues of that election had been, I was told, the new school. The ex-County Councillor had served for many years on the County Education Committee. He opened his statement by saying he wanted to put the matter in perspective, and he reviewed the development of Pentrediwaith school plans since 1900. There were, he then said, eighty condemned schools in the county, some of them worse than Pentre. In the 1930's it was decided to build Central Schools in Pentrediwaith, Trefawr and Castell; but then, as now, the national economy made cuts necessary. The Education Committee had had to make a survey of priorities. It was laid down (by higher authority, one assumed) that a Modern School (as the Central School had now become) must have at least ten teachers. Even if there were only twenty pupils to a teacher, that meant two hundred pupils. The Dafad valley could raise barely a hundred.

The speaker said that he agreed, of course, that the valley should have its own school because of its Welsh tradition. He recognized the curse of taking the children 'like sheep' out of the valley to school. He himself had worked on the Education Committee for years to get a school in the valley, and he had secured agreement that such a school should be built. It was on the list, but it was halfway down the fifth three-year period of the County Council's fifteen-year plan. In this fifth period there were fifty other projects. In any case, now in 1953 the plan was already years behind schedule. Now, however, he went on, we have an opportunity for immediate action. There was this possibility of building two huts for woodwork and sewing. This first step might pave the way for a Modern School in Pentre. But other members of the County Council would be only too glad to shelve the whole thing. He advised villagers to agree to the Education Authority's suggestions, let all the infants go to the Controlled School, and let all juniors and the eleven-plus group go to the Council School. This was necessary to enable the experimental huts to be set up.

He sat down amidst disapproving murmurs, and members of the audience got to their feet to make objections and comments. It was said that the Church School building was dirty, and that epidemics always started there and only spread later to the Council School. The sewage arrangements were primitive and ineffective. The building was old and unsafe. English-speaking and Welsh-speaking children would be mixed and the Welsh language would suffer. The playground was divided into two parts by the village street, which had become a busy road; they would be in fear for their children every time a car entered the village. All these arguments were put with some heat by the main body of the meeting, amid interruptions from the back where the Church group sat, but without immediate formal reply.

The sitting County Councillor then added his support to the County Council's view, reiterating the arguments of the ex-Councillor and recalling his own efforts on the Council. A spokesman for the Church group then got up at the back and said that he had for years attended the Church School and that it was perfectly all right. It had been going 110 years and there had not been an accident yet. He could not see why it was unsafe. Besides, he said, to a chorus of 'That's right!' from his fellows, what's it to do with those people at the front making so much noise about it? Their children were no longer at school in Pentre at all. Their children were safely installed at the Grammar School and they did not care what happened to the others who had not got in.

A representative of the Chapel people retorted that, if the Church School was so good, why did a lot of Church people send their children to the Council School? This was an accurate thrust, although it reveals the confusion which marked the whole discussion as between the Church School and the Church School building. I know of three Church families who send their children to the Council School, and there are others who wished to do so but were dissuaded.

After an hour of discussion it was agreed, on the Baptist Minister's suggestion, that the meeting should vote on a motion that they agreed to the Education Committee's proposals, but under protest. This was eventually carried by eleven votes to seven, the remaining ten (including myself) not voting. The

Minister said he would convey the views of the meeting to the Director of Education when he sent the decision. This, however, was only the beginning of the affair. The next day it was made known in the village that the Vicar had heard of the meeting, and had said he would take legal action against anyone who further slandered the Church Vestrymen by alleging that they kept the Church children in school under intolerable conditions.

At this stage an Englishman living in the village took up the matter and drafted a petition against the change. Here is the text (names omitted):

To —————— Esq.,
Director of Education.

THE REORGANIZATION OF SCHOOLS
Dear Sir,

We, the undersigned, being parents of the children of the Pentrediwaith Area, desire to express our strong objection to sending them to the Controlled School. Owing to the poor publicity of the meeting which took place on the 22nd inst. on this subject, very few parents attended. Of those parents who were present many were led astray by the remarks of ex-Councillor A, endorsed by Councillor B, to the effect that, if these proposals were not accepted, the L.E.A. would bring all other schemes here to an end and would wash their hands of all future educational facilities in the valley, which in fact amounts to intimidation.

In view of this misunderstanding and our unfortunate absence from the meeting, we submit our names as being in complete opposition to the proposal that our infants be transferred to the Controlled School, our reasons being in accordance with the sentiments expressed at the afore-mentioned meeting. We feel that no amount of money spent on this building can alter its main deficiencies, viz. the size of its classrooms and playground and its locality.

This letter of protest was taken round to selected houses with the utmost secrecy lest (I was told) the Church people should hear of it and send a counter-petition. No one was approached on the housing estate in the hopes that the originators of the petition would be able to remain anonymous. Their names, however, did leak out and their actions were interpreted, as they had feared, in terms of their kinship ties with some of the teachers in the Council School. They succeeded in collecting forty signatures in the parish after visiting outlying parts by car, and they sent the letter to the Director of Education. The Council's plan was not put into operation at the beginning of the academic year 1953-54, as had been intended originally.

At the annual general meeting of the parish council in March, 1954, which I attended, the subject was again raised by the County Councillor, who announced that the County Education Authority had applied for a loan of £6,000 to build the outbuildings for domestic science and woodwork, and that they were going ahead with transferring the infants. There were very few villagers at the meeting and no discussion on that particular point arose.

This controversy seems to me to illustrate well the characteristics of Pentrediwaith. The issues that were raised by both sides were straightforward. The smallness of the rooms, the position of the playground, and the age of the Controlled School buildings, were all verifiable faults, and in other circumstances any one of them might have served to unite the villagers against the proposals. But the village division was deeper than this, and the arguments used at the meeting were mere debating points or symbols of an underlying conflict of which this whole controversy was just one manifestation. The real controversy emerged in informal conversation and in the arguments used to rally support in private. These revealed the divisions of the village. I heard remarks like: 'I always tease my husband by threatening to send my children to the Church School where they speak English,' made by an English girl married into the village. Others said: 'It's just the Church obstructing again. They're always the same,' or: 'The Chapel people are just trying to get at the Church, they don't really care what happens to the children.'

Here was a decision that had to be made because the L.E.A. demanded action from the villagers. The villagers were reluctant to have their divisions exposed formally and in public. The County Councillor called in a former Councillor from another village to put the L.E.A.'s case. Although he later contributed to the discussion, and spoke in favour of the proposals, he let the main support for them come from an outsider.

The resolution passed was a compromise: 'We agree under protest.' And a long covering letter with the technical arguments against the proposal was sent with it. When opposition was finally organized the vital steps were taken by a member of an outside group, a middle-class Englishman married into a Welsh Nonconformist village family. He drafted the petition, I (another outsider) typed it, and he took it round to people he was advised by villagers would sign it.

So, although there was an indication of disunity at the meeting, neither side publicly and formally committed themselves to an outright statement that the others were wrong. The public quarrel was between two strangers, and on the surface the village hardly appeared to be involved. Although Church and Chapel members of the same family had different opinions, the village did not divide into hostile camps. Each villager's attitude was determined not by his or her consideration of the advantages and disadvantages of the proposed change, but by his or her position in village society, and in particular by Church or Chapel membership. It was alleged with truth in discussion that some Church people preferred to send their children to the Council School. This added a complication to the attitude of those Church people who would have liked to send their children there, but hesitated to do so for fear of offending yet other Church people. These welcomed the County Council's suggestion as a solution of their personal difficulties.

Moreover, the fact that villagers would not openly underline the Church-Chapel division does not mean that they were unconscious of it. We have seen that they expressed it freely in private. This 'two-faced' behaviour should not be interpreted, as it is by outsiders in Pentre and by the English in Wales generally, as mere hypocrisy. As long as the split in the village is not openly revealed and made public, life can be carried on as if the split was not there.

Other situations arose in Pentre where this device was employed. One of the most striking of these was the village reaction to the suggestions of a woman who developed paranoid delusions. One of these was that there was a conspiracy to rob her of her furniture. The furniture was carried to 'safety' to the house of a villager. This operation was carried out with great secrecy and at night but, in fact, with the full knowledge of most of the villagers. The house where much of the furniture was deposited was next door to that of the alleged ringleader of the suspected 'burglars', and the neighbours were on good terms. The woman concerned wished to remain on good terms with her neighbour but realized that looking after someone's furniture for the apparent reason that one believes that one's neighbour's husband is contemplating burglary, is not conducive to good relations between close neighbours. She therefore decided to hide the furniture and keep her sheltering it secret. All the women who visited the house, including the neighbour, made no public reference to her secret, although I discovered at various times in private conversation that they, and indeed most other villagers, knew what had happened from the very beginning. By acting as if no one knew, the woman and her neighbour remained on good terms, and the whole story was not publicly revealed until a month or two later when the unfortunate paranoid was finally certified and entered a mental hospital.

Similarly, on a larger scale an appearance of unity can be obtained by a refusal openly to recognize rifts in society that are privately known to exist. In critical situations such as arise when decisions must be taken, a division of interests normally hidden may come to the surface. It is at these times, at least in Pentrediwaith, that strangers and outsiders play their social role most fully.

I started my discussion of Pentrediwaith, as a community or social system by describing the division between Outsiders and Pentre People. This, I argued, was based on economic class and complicated by language and religion. I have tried to show how the internal divisions amongst villagers, mediated by the same kind of differences, complicate the political organization. I have analysed, as a secondary theme, the role of strangers in certain political situations in enabling the villagers to preserve their social unity in the face of this internal disunity. Social groupings maintain their own cohesion by bringing in a stranger both to act as a scapegoat and as a reminder to group members that they belong and must maintain their solidarity against others who do not.

Thus divisions which arose out of the course of economic

history and the relations of Wales and England influence the political relations of Pentrediwaith villagers with the outside world. The same sort of divisions, and the same mechanisms to overcome and emphasize them which act in this external political situation, are carried over into the internal politics which surround the organization of recreational activity.

IV

THE POLITICS OF RECREATION

IN the last chapter we saw that the interest aroused within the village by the parish council and its affairs does not extend to what the parish councillors do outside the village. Villagers are indifferent as to whether parish councillors attend the meetings of the County Association or not. Although the parish council acts from time to time for the village as a whole and negotiates on behalf of the village with outside powers, it is not a symbol of village unity and cohesion against the outside world.

During 1953 the village football club provided such a symbol but this was not, of course, its only function in village life. The fact that the outside prestige of the village would be judged by the football club's public appearances did, however, have the effect of giving football a central place in village social activity. In the village details of the internal struggles of the football, flower show and fête committees were of paramount importance, trivial though they may seem from outside. This is generally true of village affairs, as is demonstrated if one attempts to read a local newspaper from an area with which one is not familiar; its repetition of detail soon palls on the outsider. Furthermore, internal village events provide a private time scale for villagers which a visitor soon adopts. When, on a brief visit from the field, I read a paper to the Manchester Seminar, my colleagues laughed at my dating of events. I used such phrases as : 'Just before the Carnival', 'after the Coronation Tea', and 'before the Sheep-dog Trials'. To me, still immersed in Pentrediwaith, the joke had to be explained.

Football is only one social activity which brings the village into contact with other villages, but in 1953 it happened to be the most important. There were, even then, others. Eisteddfod 'parties' of singers and reciters attended local Eisteddfodau, drama groups performed in other villages. In other years there was a choir and a brass band which travelled about the country-side to give performances. Such trips enlarged the villagers' acquaintanceships and emphasized to other villages the existence and prowess of Pentre people.

Football brings other village teams in, as well as sending Pentre villagers out. This bringing-in is also achieved by the sheep-dog trials which have been held annually for over fifty years, by the flower show, and in 1953 by the carnival. Sectional groups within the village also brought visitors in. There was a performance at the Baptist Chapel of *The Messiah* by a choir from outside and debating teams were exchanged by the Baptist Young People's societies of Pentre and other villages. All these activities, however, which at different times have made Pentrediwaith, or groups of its villagers, known and praised outside the valley, were overshadowed in 1953 by the activities of Pentrediwaith Amateur Football Club and associated events in the village.

Association football is the established sport of this part of North Wales. I cannot say how it came to be so, for this is a problem soluble only by historical research. But once established, it is possible to see some of its advantages over other possible recreations. It is a sport, in contrast to sheep-dog trials and slate-splitting competitions, which has a more than specialist appeal.[1] The equipment needed for football is relatively inexpensive and the preparation for a game or a competition is not very arduous. The season is long, from August to May, but leaves the summer free for gardening and holiday activities. Football is very nearly an all-weather game. The Welsh Football Association and the Welsh National League provide a framework in which a village team can take its place. Since this framework exists and other villages have teams it is considered that each important village should be represented in its local League in order to maintain its prestige. The national organization takes (or should take) much of the burden off local organizations since it fixes the length of the

---

[1] It should not be thought that the handling of sheep-dogs is a skill practised only by shepherds. Pentrediwaith's great exponent of the skill was a quarryman. His son, who carries on the family tradition, works in a factory.

H

season, arranges the fixtures, and lays down the rules. The
League provides referees and specifies kick-off times. The
village has merely to muster eleven players and some officials
and provide a pitch. The rest is provided from above. Finally,
association football is above all the British national game.
Whatever local and class allegiances there may be to rugby
union or rugby league, league and county cricket, or to
tennis and still more localized games like marbles, bowls,
darts or archery, association football is the one sporting interest
and topic of conversation which can cut across all class and
regional boundaries.

Pentrediwaith's football club provides participation in this
national game for both spectators and players. The spectators
keep their eye in for North Wales Coast matches and the Welsh
Amateur Cup, for Third Division (North) League matches
and cup-ties and for Internationals and the First Division
farther afield. To have a village team, especially when composed of local lads, fosters the fanatical partisanship which
gives savour even to professional League football in the towns
and gives Pentre football an intense importance in the village.
The honour of the village and its place in the outside world
are at stake in each game and in the day-to-day conduct of
the club.

The players enjoy the game, the exercise and the local prestige. They sometimes hope to advance to Oldham or Wrexham
in the Third Division or to the better North Wales clubs. One
or two Pentrediwaith youths in recent years have had trials
for Manchester City. It is not forgotten in Pentrediwaith that
the fabulous Billy Meredith, Welsh International and player
for both Manchester City and United, came from a village in
North Wales.

The fact that everyone in the village, almost without exception, is pleased when Pentrediwaith distinguishes itself on the
football field does not mean that the village unites, in amity
and co-operation, to make the village football team a success.
The very intensity of interest that the game arouses leads also
to divergencies of opinion. Committees split into overtly and
latently hostile groups, often along lines predetermined by
family dislikes or by insults incurred in entirely different situations but carried over into the organization of recreation.

The divergent groups are not congruent with those already discussed in political organization, but they overlap and cut across them. Church and Chapel members are, for example, to be found on both sides of a football controversy.

The Chapels do not actively oppose football although the more austere deacons and ministers may regard it as a frivolous occupation. Many of the activities which were associated with the raising of funds for the football club were very much opposed by the Baptist minister in Pentrediwaith. His opposition to dances, whist-drives and raffles did not, however, seem to discourage his members from participation in these events, or even from taking an active part in their organization. The Anglican vicar was an active supporter of the club and a vice-president; he contributed generously to its finances and, whenever he was free to do so, attended its matches. Considerations of Church and Chapel did not enter to any important extent into the deliberations of the committee or its initial election.

Thus the 1952-3 football committee had a Baptist chairman and treasurer and a Church secretary; five of the rest of the committee were Church and seven were Chapel. The Supporters' Club Committee, in the same season, had a Church chairman and secretary and a Baptist treasurer; six of the rest were Church and seven were Chapel. In the football committee on which I served in season 1953-4 the chairman, secretary and treasurer were all Chapel members. There were two English outsiders, two other Church and three other Chapel members amongst the regular attenders. The active supporters' committee members in the 1953-4 Season had a Church chairman and secretary and a Baptist treasurer; six of the ordinary members were Chapel members and one was Church.

Both Church and Chapel members were equally shocked when a sweepstake was suggested. The only difference in behaviour which arose from denominational differences was that Chapel members were more likely to miss meetings because of the demands of other activities organized by the Chapel. Generally speaking, membership of a particular denomination did not seem to me directly significant in determining behaviour within the football and supporters' committees or in other activities connected with football.

When differences had arisen along other lines, however, denomination was sometimes used, in private discussion, as the last straw added to an already heavy indictment: 'Those Church people are always the same.' The effect of denominational differences was then to help in fixing individuals in their social positions in the village by adding another consideration to the individual's unstated problem: 'Can I co-operate with X in this matter?'

The social divisions which are significant to the organization of football are apparent when the structure of the football and supporters' clubs is examined and when the sequence of events during 1953 is described. There are in Pentrediwaith two clubs whose primary concern is, or was until mid-1953, the carrying on of football. They are the Football Club and the Football Supporters' Club. We shall see that the clash of interested groups within the individual clubs is mitigated by the fact that after a serious dispute the defeated group withdraws from the committee and continues its criticism from outside. Some members of these defeated groups do not stop at criticism but actively work against the interests of the club they have left. Thus, during 1953, notices of forthcoming matches and the chosen team were mysteriously torn from the tree where they had been fixed. Other such examples will appear in the following pages. The withdrawal of support for a social activity by groups of villagers eventually results in the death of that social activity. The football club reached this pass in 1953-4 and did not survive into the next season. From what villagers told me it appears that this fate also overtook the brass band and the male voice choir, but I have not documentary historical material to confirm this.

Whatever the internal divisions in the football and in the supporters' club, the major division in this context is between the *football* and the *supporters*—that is, between the men and the women. This was clear not only in the progress of the carnival-football dispute, and in the proceedings of the carnival committee itself, but also in the daily behaviour and conversation of villagers. For example, when particular men failed to attend whist drives organized by the supporters, they were criticized very severely by the women. 'Where would the football club be without the women to make money for it?' members of the football committee were asked. The usual reply, not often given directly, was to ask what the women would find to do if they had no football club to support. On one occasion a man who was very active in the football club attended a supporters' whist drive after threats by the women to withdraw support from the football club if he did not. He took first prize. He regarded this as 'one in the eye' for the supporters and told the story to other men with great mutual enjoyment. The whole incident only served to intensify the resentment of the women.

The argument about whist-drive attendance was constantly repeated between different men and women. It is of course true that in actual fact many men enjoyed the whist drives. Furthermore, some women not only came to watch home matches but even travelled with the team to away games. Although such people were not regarded as abnormal and women supporters were expected to attend at least home matches, villagers behaved as if football itself was an activity which was of interest and benefit only to men. On the other hand social activities like dances and whist drives, organized to raise funds for the football club, were spoken of as a chore that the women carried out for the benefit of the men. Both these views were put forward in the first place by the women, but they had secured their acceptance, at least in public, by the men. In fact, as I have suggested and will demonstrate, if football had not existed to provide a reason for organizing events, some other excuse would have been found.[1]

It is necessary to make a brief digression here to describe the very strong sense of obligations of reciprocity that pervades Pentrediwaith life. The relations of the supporters' club and the football club were coloured by this attitude to mutual obligations. The supporters' club gave £70 to the football club in season 1951-2, £50 in season 1952-3, and £60 in 1953-4. But these gifts were not free of obligation. In Pentrediwaith it is not considered comfortable to receive a free gift. A gift creates an obligation, which must be met. This principle extends from the slightest transaction between individuals to the dealings of

[1] At the 1954 carnival, which I attended, it was announced that the carnival was in aid of a children's playing field, the football team having gone out of existence.

corporate groups.[1] To a Pentre villager getting something for nothing from another villager is not an achievement, it is a disgrace. Thus when a woman had taken morning tea with her sister daily for two or three weeks she felt it necessary to bring a little tea in a paper bag as recompense. A young man invited to watch the Hungary-England football match on television was very doubtful about accepting the invitation lest he incurred thereby an obligation that he had not the means to repay. This scrupulousness does not always extend to outsiders. When a publican installed a television set in his bar he found it increased attendance but reduced his takings; even regular drinkers found the television so absorbing that they forgot their obligation to drink as well as watch. Although 'co-operation' on the scale described by Rees and Huw Evans[2] is not carried out in Pentre some villagers have arrangements to help local farmers at critical times in the farm year. They are rewarded for these services by their meals and in kind. For example, one family who keep chickens are given corn in return for their harvest services. Those who help with potato-lifting receive sacks of potatoes. When I coached a farmer's son in English, I did not of course receive payment for my services, but I seldom left the farm without supper and never without a rabbit, a dozen eggs, a bag of potatoes or some similar gift.

The wife of a villager who did local building jobs shared out her food registrations (under rationing) between two of the four village grocers and bought bread from a third. She had milk delivered by both village milkmen and bought additional bread from the baker. Her husband in return received some of each tradesman's building work which they shared out in the same way. When in 1953 advertising space on the carnival programme was sold, one women shopkeeper misunderstood and did not buy any. When the programme appeared and her name was not mentioned, she not only refused to attend the carnival or help it in any way, but also tore up a copy of the programme offered to her by a seller on the village's main street. Despite Chapel rivalry, members of

---

[1] Pentre is of course not unique in this; cf. Mauss, M., *The Gift: Forms and Functions of Exchange in Archaic Societies*, translated by Ian Cunnison, Cohen & West, 1953.

[2] Rees, ch. viii, pp. 91 ff.; Evans, Huw, *The Gorse Glen* ('Cwm Eithin'), Brython Press, Liverpool, 1948.

different Chapels and the Church support each other's functions, and no door-to-door collectors in the village are turned away empty-handed.

Reciprocity has helped the village to keep going in times of difficulty, and has united the village and its participant groups into a coherent whole; but when it is not observed, or is believed not to have been observed, reciprocity can divide as well as unite. Thus, in the relations of the football and supporters' clubs reciprocity plays an important part. They are united by a common interest in keeping the football club going: when this fails, as it first began to do in 1952, breaches of reciprocal obligation widen the gap.

In theory the whole village are members of both clubs. Both clubs have, or should have, annual general meetings which all villagers are entitled to attend. In fact very few villagers outside the committees do attend the public meetings of either; when a villager refers to the supporters' club or the football club he usually means the committee. But the committee are regarded as representing the whole village; like the parish council, they are subjected to constant informal criticism which, as in the case of the parish council, is made irritatingly more effective by its refusal to come into the open at public meetings.

Pentre people have other infallible sanctions to keep these committees under control. If villagers stay away from events organized by the committee, they gain the double satisfaction, first, of placing the committee in an embarrassing position financially and, secondly, of being able to blame it for the plight into which it has in fact been forced by public action. Villagers who first oppose and then kill an event in this way can and do say: 'We told you so!' Thus although only a very small number of villagers are active in the day-to-day running of the football club, these few receive informal advice and criticism without stint from the majority. The duties of the committee members, although light if shared by many, can become very arduous, and Saturday-night criticism is not the least of the sacrifices of personal freedom and other discomforts involved in accepting office. There is little open competition for places on the committees (although there may be a struggle to displace officers). Members once elected rarely resign during the year. This is because committee members themselves accept the values of the community and fear both the downfall of the club and the blame and loss of face the committee members would suffer if they allowed football to die out. At the time of the annual general meeting, however, they do succeed in finding excuses to leave. Different officers have led the club each year in the three seasons 1951-2, 1952-3 and 1953-4. Those of 1953-4 declined to carry on another year, and the club no longer functions.

In some committees there is an almost irresistible social pressure against resigning. One woman told me how she became ill and wanted to give up her village social commitments. When she announced that she was leaving the British Legion (women's section) committee the secretary became very cold in her attitude towards her, and the would-be resigner stayed on to prevent ill-feeling. She also stayed on the supporters' committee because the secretary said he would resign if she did. Then other members said they would not stay if the secretary went. By this time the woman felt that public opinion was against her, someone said she was trying wantonly to destroy the whole club, and she gave in. Not until three years later, when her ill-health was apparent, did she succeed in resigning. Her case was not untypical.

THE FOOTBALL CLUB

The football committee met once or twice a week to choose the team for the following Saturday and to transact any other business as it arose. The other business often concerned disputes with the League over the non-fulfilment of obligations on both sides. Committee members were expected to travel, at their own expense, on the bus which carried the team to away matches on alternate Saturdays. One of the committee acted as linesman and another as trainer. In addition, members of the committee had to play occasionally as substitutes for players who had failed to turn up. For home games the field had to be marked with lime, the grass cut occasionally and thistles uprooted.

These last three jobs were all arduous and unpleasant. Usually the lime was applied by hand in powdered form. One just filled a bucket with the powder and sprinkled it in handfuls

along the lines (or what seemed to be the lines). This job
ruined one's clothes, dried one's throat and stung one's hands.
It was very expensive in lime and on windy days the marker
appeared to have been rolling in flour. Later in the 1953-4
season the club acquired a mechanical marker which employed
a lime solution, but the condition of the field reduced its
efficiency and made it difficult to use. When there was snow
on the ground sawdust was used for marking. Other preparations on the field, which was a pasture during the week, were
also arduous and unpleasant. The grass was cut with scythes
or even sickles and mole hills had to be flattened. Occasionally
turf displaced by pigs had to be replaced. The players had to
take their chance of avoiding the cowpats as the committee
had no inclination to remove them.

The nets had to be placed in position before home games and
the balls inflated and fetched to the pitch. Two committee
members had to collect the money at the gate, while another
fetched tea from the village at half-time and paid the referee's
fee and expenses. After the game the nets had to be taken down
again. This was a wet, cold, dirty and awkward job because
the nets were tied to the cross-bar with creosoted string and
there was no step-ladder. Someone else had to collect the
players' dirty clothes and see that they were washed and in
good condition for the following week. Finally, according to
Football Association rules, the committee is also responsible
for the safety of the referee; this is not always a light burden.
Thus the committee members had chores to perform as well
as decisions to make, and some of them, like marking the field,
were both time-consuming and tedious. These jobs were the
prerogative of committee members only and the suggestion
at committee meetings that others be 'allowed' (sic) to help was
at first strongly opposed, although it was eventually adopted.

As the Welsh language served to determine the class composition of the parish council, so the existence of chores limited to
some extent the economic class status of members of the
football committee. Excluding myself, all those who served as
ordinary committee members in seasons 1951-2, 1952-3, and
1953-4 were working men. Even the officers were not far
removed. The chairmen during the first two seasons were in
fact employers of labour in a very small way, but they worked

themselves side by side with their employees. The vice-chairman, the manager of the local Co-operative Stores, helped each week to take the nets down and to collect money at the gate, but he was implicitly excused from the various tasks of preparation of the field. In season 1953-4, the chairman, secretary and treasurer were all white-collar workers, and on several occasions one of them complained to me that cutting grass was not the sort of work he was accustomed to; it made him feel, he said, 'like a bloody navvy'.

Although the committee had, in theory, a hierarchic structure, its leaders lacked authority. Decisions had to be taken in accordance with 'the principle of unanimity'. Consequently necessary tasks were frequently not performed. On one occasion only seven players turned up to an away match and the linesman, trainer and other committee members played. Once the pitch was not marked at all and the referee refused to start until at least some of the salient points had been indicated. Home matches almost invariably started late and the club usually had to pay a fine at the rate of sixpence per minute to the League. Sometimes the half-time tea did not materialize or the referee remained unpaid. I do not remember a single Saturday when everything went off without a hitch.

Apart from their direct responsibilities to carry out the tasks necessary to run the football club, committee members had the incidental duties of attending social functions organized by the supporters' club in the village and of buying the raffle tickets which members of the supporters' club take round at every home match. Alleged failure to fulfil these obligations gave rise to continual controversy.

The committee which carried out all these functions had as the senior official in its formal structure a president. He was expected to give a handsome donation to the club but not to preside. In 1952-3 the president was the Welsh-speaking publican of one of the three village pubs. It appears that he did actually preside over informal inquests held in his bar. He gave a £5 donation.[1] In 1953-4 he declined to continue in office, and his place was taken by the English-speaking

---

[1] The costs of running a football club even on a small scale are surprisingly high. In 1952-3 the club had a turnover of over £260. In the previous season it had one of over £200. The figures for 1953-4 are not available.

proprietor of the principal village grocer's shop. He was a newcomer to the village and he did on one occasion preside at a committee meeting but, trained in English public school 'rugger', he apparently did not feel at home and did not come again. He remained a generous supporter of the club.

Next to the president were ten or eleven vice-presidents—local gentry, shopkeepers and publicans who owed their position to their ability and willingness to help financially. Below the vice-presidents was the club committee proper with a chairman, a vice-chairman (representing the Women's Supporters' Club of which, though a man, he was chairman), a secretary, a treasurer and ordinary committee members. Most committee members in season 1953-4 were ex-players for the club. Committee members who still play are not encouraged because of the obvious difficulty of discussing their performances. One man who was very keen on the football club refused an invitation to serve on the committee on the grounds that it would prejudice his chances of being chosen to play for the club. The team captain was an ex-officio committee member but never attended. Only three members of the committee had never played for the club: myself, a Londoner who had come to live in the village and worked in a nearby colliery, and the 'supporters' representative'.

The membership of the football committee was exceptional at the beginning of season 1953-4 in that there were five coal-miners serving on it. This was probably the result of disputes in season 1952-3 between the miner secretary and other committee members. It was, however, very characteristic of Pentrediwaith committees (other than those concerned with local government) that their membership did not consist of isolated individuals but of groups united by kinship or other ties. These groups voted, and from time to time resigned, as units. The miners' group in the 1953-4 committee was one example of this; in the previous season an informal drinking-group led by the chairman was another. This latter group resigned as a body at the end of season 1952-3, but when things were going badly in 1953-4 offered to come back as a group. Their offer was accepted, but they changed their minds before the next meeting. When the miner secretary (12) resigned in 1953 he resigned alone, but he continued to discuss the affairs of the club and to exert an influence on them through his informal relations with the miners who remained. One by one during the season they also resigned or just ceased to attend.

The new secretary, Humphrey Biggs (6), also collected a group of this kind by pressing his father and brothers into service during a period when it was difficult to find people to do the necessary jobs. Long before this, however, villagers were blaming the football club's lack of success on the fact that it had got into the control of 'those Biggs'.[1]

There was an opposing group within the committee, but conflicts actually within the football club never became very intense. The crises within the club were acute but not chronic, since they usually led to a conflicting group's resigning or becoming inactive. Consequently, as we have seen, by the end of 1953 there was scarcely any one left prepared to serve on the football committee. Even the last of the eligible strangers, that is, those sufficiently humble to do manual work, had departed. As I have suggested, this seems a characteristic development.

The changes in the committee during 1953-4 demonstrate this process of reducing the numbers available to serve, but they are linked also to changes in the other, and perhaps most important, section of the club—the players. The tendency in the three seasons under review was for the players to be drawn less and less from Pentrediwaith itself. In some games in 1953 there was only one villager in the team, yet I was told that when the game was first revived after the war the team consisted entirely of Pentre players. The first post-war team included three pairs of brothers all from this village. The twenty-six registered players in season 1952-3 included thirteen from the village. No records were kept of which of these actually played, but from my own knowledge of the players and from discussions with villagers I can say that five of the Pentre players on the list would be chosen only if it were unavoidable owing to the absence of other outside players. While I was in Pentrediwaith I kept a weekly record of the gate-money and raffle money, who was chosen and who played, which I present in the following table.

[1] The numbers in brackets after names and officials refer to Diagram II on p. 118.

Table II

Number of Villagers
in Team

Week	Gate £ s. d.	Raffle £ s. d.	Chosen	Played	Result
1	4 6 0	1 4 8	5	8	Lost 9—1
2	AWAY		8	8	Lost 2—1
3	5 0 0	1 15 0	3	3	Lost 7—2
4	AWAY		3	5	Lost 7—1
5	CARNIVAL				
6	3 0 0	1 13 0	2	3	Lost 7—1
7	3 0 1	1 10 6	3	3	Won 4—3*
8	AWAY		3	4	Lost 5—2
9	AWAY		3	4	Lost 11—2
10	AWAY		3	3	Won 5—3
11	2 10 0	19 0	3	3	Lost 7—3
12	AWAY		2	2	Lost 6—0
13	1 19 8	10 0	3	3	Lost 5—3
14	2 11 0	13 6	2	2	Lost 3—0
15	AWAY		1	1	Lost 8—4
16	1 5 0	No Raffle	1	2	Lost 4—2

* Disallowed.

The post-war founders of the club remained in office as chairman and treasurer for five years until the end of the 1951-2 season. The secretary at that time was a young bank clerk who has since emigrated to Australia. By the end of the 1951-2 season the club was well established, and the question first arose which has bedevilled its activities ever since. The committee were divided as to the aims of the club. Should it be just to provide football for local boys to play and local men to watch, or should it go all out for the championship of its division in the Welsh National League? A necessary corollary of the latter decision was bringing outsiders into the team, as by 1952 it was already clear that local players on their own could not reach the required standard.[1] Decision was reached in favour of all-out competition in the League and the chairman,

[1] According to Kempe, J., 'A Pilot Survey of Much Marcle', *The Sociological Review*, xli, 1949, Section 1, a similar problem arose in Much Marcle. This, however, was a flourishing community from the economic point of view and they solved it by having two teams. A similar solution was not possible in Pentrediwaith because of the economic situation.

Tom, and treasurer, Philip (1), champions of the opposing viewpoint, retired from the club.

I was not, of course, in Pentrediwaith at this time, but from conversation with villagers I have formed some impression of these early post-war years. The team was at first not only local but also strong, but its members were near the end of their playing careers. Some of these players were on the committee in 1953 but had retired from active playing. The young men in the original team have left the district to work elsewhere. Unlike season 1953-4, the early years were years of success, but the committee was nevertheless not always at peace. There were even then resignations and quarrels, the fruits of some of which were still apparent in 1953.

At the end of 1951-2 the team stood third in its League Division. They had up to that time played on a field adjoining the Castell road, between the Council school and the minister's house. This had the disadvantage that it was easy to watch the game from the outside without going into the field at all. In this way villagers could avoid both the entrance payment and getting their feet wet. The danger to the club's revenues arising from this situation was partly met by having a collection among the non-paying spectators, and the response to this expedient was improved by having a policeman to make the collection in his helmet. The new committee, with Charley (12) as secretary, moved from this field to a more remote pitch a little way outside the village and surrounded by other fields. On this new site only paying spectators could see.

This move had its disadvantages. At the old field watching football on Saturday was often a casual affair. People on their way to and from the village had to pass the field. Sometimes they stopped for a moment to watch, became interested and stayed. The general uproar during an exciting game could be heard from all parts of the village and attracted people to the ground. This gave rise to an amusing incident during one particularly hard-fought game with a team regarded as a traditional rival. On this Saturday afternoon a villager going off to shoot rabbits was on his way up the hill leading to the church when he heard a particularly loud roar from the football ground. He returned to the village to see what was going on, became more interested in watching the game than in continuing his shoot and remained. The referee made decisions which the visitors did not approve of and they later complained to the Welsh F.A. At the inquiry which followed the visitors' officials insisted that not only had the Pentrediwaith crowd been aggressive and threatening but that one of them had even brought a shotgun to intimidate the referee.

At the field used in 1953 to come and watch the game was always a deliberate act. No one passed the field or visited it except for the specific purpose of watching football. Some villagers felt, I believe with reason, that by moving in this way outside the village physically, the football club was also isolating itself to some extent from the social life of the village. Only real enthusiasts would follow a losing team in such circumstances. In my opinion, it is highly probable that this was a factor in producing the falling off of feminine interest in the game, and all that that implied in the loss of financial support. For the women of Pentre were often busy on Saturday, as on any other afternoon. For them the moving of the field from a central point in the village to right outside was almost equivalent to moving it to Castell or Tonmawr. The move made football virtually inaccessible. Many women lost interest also when the team came to be predominantly composed of outsiders. The combination of a 'foreign' team and a distant field adopted by the committee at the outset of season 1952-3 brought into the open the already existing conflict of interests between the men of the football club and the women of the supporters' club. As I have suggested, in Pentrediwaith, particularly now that most men go away to work, the full support of the women is crucial for the success of any activity.

At this critical point in the external relations of the football club a new secretary, Charley (12), a coal miner, took office. This internal change had significance beyond a mere change of personalities. Previously secretary, chairman and treasurer worked together with the committee to choose the team. The secretary had the responsibility of notifying the team and therefore had no vote in committee on the selection or placing of the team. I often heard him in 1953 arguing with players and pointing out that he was not responsible for changes in the team, but that the committee was. This worked in practice as well as in theory as long as the team was local. The secretary at the outset had no more power than other committee members, and perhaps had less. Furthermore, he was a player himself and a young man, whereas Tom, the chairman at this time, was much older and used to authority. Tom was Welsh-speaking, Baptist, and a builder who worked beside, as well as gave orders to, his men. He was sufficiently outside and above the group he led to exert authority over them, but sufficiently similar in outlook to be listened to, and worked with, by the other committee members in close co-operation.

When the principle of a team of outsiders was accepted, the secretary's position changed. The village club had to compete with other local teams for the services of even local players. Competition for players from farther afield was still more intense. It usually came about, therefore, that players brought in from other districts were in fact either workmates or friends of workmates of the secretary. The relative position of the secretary and the rest of the committee was now reversed. The secretary no longer merely notified the players chosen by the committee; he now nominated players to the committee, secured their selection, and was the committee's only means of communication with them. If a secretary says that X will not play inside-left, and X is a village boy, the statement is easily checked. But if X comes from a relatively distant town and works at the next laboratory bench to the secretary, he is difficult to get hold of for questioning. The secretary was in fact invested with power, and this inevitably led him into conflict with the committee.

I know that this situation existed in season 1952-3 but I cannot give detailed examples of it. In season 1953-4 there were many examples. One player from outside whom the committee wished to play half-back was said to have refused to play anything but inside-forward. Only when the secretary was ill one week was contact made with him by post and his position changed. On another occasion it was decided not to drop a player who was getting old and replace him by another. Both players involved were outsiders from the same works. The change was made, despite the committee, 'at the older player's wish'. The committee had no opportunity to check this in time.

The officers for the 1952-3 season, apart from the secretary, resigned at the end of the season on the ostensible grounds of other more pressing work. They said in private it was because the secretary was too domineering and chose his own team. In season 1953-4 one group resigned from the committee for the same reason after an open discussion in committee.

Pentre villagers participate in village activities not as individuals but in small informal groups composed of from three to six individuals. These groups join, participate and resign from committees *as* groups. In this context this group behaviour has two results: firstly, the secretary collects his own group of supporters in the committee, as Charley did with the miners; secondly, the secretary's power is increased by the fact that the players also participate in informal groups amongst themselves.[1] Given that the players come from the secretary's place of work and that they are comparatively unknown to the rest of the committee, he is able to tell the committee that if Y is dropped from the team as the committee wishes, X and Z will not play because X, Y and Z always spend Saturday afternoons together. Further, since such groups overlap, if Z does not play, A will not, and Pentre may lose B on A's account. At one point in season 1953-4, two players from a First Division team of the Welsh National League transferred to Pentrediwaith. The Pentrediwaith committee members were naturally curious as to why they wished to leave a winning First Division team for a losing Second Division one. The secretary replied that they did so to be with two of their workmates and friends already playing for Pentrediwaith. On another occasion two Trefawr brothers who had previously played for Pentre were going to return to Pentre because they objected to the dropping by Trefawr of their friend, the Trefawr centre-half. Unfortunately for Pentre the proposed substitute

---

[1] One of the rules of the Welsh Football Association is that an amateur player cannot be a registered player for more than one club under its jurisdiction. There is therefore a struggle at the beginning of the season to persuade good players to sign for one's club before another club succeeds in 'signing' them. During the season it is possible to get players transferred from one club to another within the League, but only on a player's own initiative. It is also possible to sign players from clubs affiliated to other Football Associations. A club in the Shropshire F.A. succeeded in enticing the Pentre Captain to play for them on a few occasions in 1953. Another Pentre player refused to play for Pentre while Biggs was in power and went to a Shropshire club of his own accord.

I

centre-half broke his arm and could not play, so the three friends stayed in First Division Trefawr.

Thus whether he abused his power (as committee members alleged) or not, the secretary had power, once the principle of the outside team was accepted, to dominate team selection. This brought him into conflict with the rest of the committee. During this conflict he might, and did in Pentrediwaith in both 1952-3 and 1953-4, develop his own group of adherents. The chairman, if he were effective, would be outside both the secretary's group and their opponents. The role of the 'stranger' will apear in the detailed discussion of the events of season 1953-4.

Diagram II

FOOTBALL COMMITTEE MEMBERS' ATTENDANCE RECORD

(Six of previous year's committee re-elected but did not attend.)

1 *Weeks* 13 *Weeks* 26	Total	Committee
XXXOOOOXOOOXXOOOXOXX : : : : :	10	*Chairman:* Philip (1)
OOXXXXXOXXXOXXXOXXXXXX : :	19	*Vice-Chairman:* Percy (2)
XXXXXXXXXOXXXXXOOXXXXXXXX	23	*Treasurer:* Timothy (3)
XXXXXXXXXXXXXXXXXXXOX : : :	22	Myself (4)
XXXXXXXXXXXXXXXXXXXXXXX	26	Arnold (5)
XXXXXXXXXOXXXXXXXOOXXXXXXX	23	*Secretary:* Humphrey (6)
XXXXXXXXOXXXXXXXXXXX : : :	22	M ⎱ English Miner (7)
XXXXXXXXXXXXXXOXXXXOXXX : : :	21	I ⎪ William (8)
XXXXXXXXXXXXXXXOXXOOXX : : : : :	18	N ⎬ Edmond (9)
XXXXXXXXXXX : : : : : : : : : : : :	12	E ⎪ Adam (10)
XXXXXXXXXXOX : : : : : : : : : : : :	11	R ⎱ Edgar (11)
XX :	2	S *Secretary:* Charley (12)
XX :	2	Farmer (13)

William (8) and Edgar (11) are brothers. A third brother was the team Captain and Humphrey's (6) best friend. Percy (2) and Arnold (5) work together as manager and assistant in the local 'Co-op'. Edmond (9) has a brother, Edward—numbered (25) in Diagrams III and IV. Edward (25) played in the team until his friend Charley (12) resigned. Percy (2) is also Chairman of the Supporters. Philip (1) and Timothy (3) are bank clerks. Humphrey (6) also has an office job.

X denotes attendance, O denotes absence, from a particular meeting.

When the founders left the football club in 1952 and Charley (12) became its secretary, there were fifteen committee members. The chairman led one group which I shall call the Green group: it had ten members. In addition there were three older men, a miner friend of the secretary, and Humphrey Biggs (6), whose father was one of the Green group. Despite their resignations six of the Green group were elected on to the committee again in season 1953-4. Not one of them attended a single meeting. Nor did they attend the general meeting which opened the 1953-4 season. At this meeting Charley (12) was re-elected secretary, and Philip (1), one of the founders, was recalled to the committee by being elected chairman in his absence. Five miners, (7, 8, 9, 10, 11), friends of Charley, one of them an Englishman (7), were elected on to the general committee, and Humphrey Biggs (6) was re-elected as well. Timothy (3), the brother of the original secretary, was elected treasurer. He played for the club and was a bank clerk in Bigtown. Percy (2), the manager of the Co-operative Stores and chairman of the supporters' club, was elected to represent the latter. Arnold (5), Percy's assistant in the stores and an ex-player, was also elected. Finally I myself (4) was elected to the committee on the stated grounds that I always attended matches and had been keen enough to attend the annual general meeting. I pointed out that I attended out of duty, but this was not considered a bar to my election if I were willing, which of course I was.

This then was the committee which started the season 1953-4. The decline in local support and in the local composition of the team which had started in 1952 was reaching its climax and the season began, as it was to go on, in conflict.

The chairman, Philip (1), was no exception to the rule of stranger chairmen of committees, but even he did not remain active long. For one excuse or another he stayed away from the committee meetings; he ended by breaking with the club on the grounds that he had too many enemies on the committee. Philip was Welsh-speaking and the clerk at the village branch of a national bank (a two-man establishment). He attended the Baptist Chapel but had no home in the village. He lived at the hotel and often went home for week-ends to his own village. He was previously the club goalkeeper, and had been treasurer when the club was revived after the war. Percy (2), the vice-chairman, who presided more often than the chairman, was, as has been mentioned, the manager of the 'Co-op' and an English-speaking Welshman born in a nearby village. In the absence of both these men I was usually asked to take the chair.

As we have seen, the founder-chairman, Tom, was not an outsider, as (although he was born in a neighbouring parish), he had many relations in the village, spoke Welsh, attended the Baptist Chapel and was a parish councillor. He was nevertheless set a little apart, as he had never worked in the quarry and was in 1953 an employer of labour himself on a very small scale. Until 1926 he ran a family coal merchant's business which he had inherited. The second chairman, Green, had a similar background and ran his own small business. It was not until crisis was reached in 1953 that strangers were drafted on to the football committee in force. Indeed, the first comments of villagers when the new committee was announced were to the effect that it seemed that village football was to be run by 'foreigners' that year.

In the interim period between seasons 1952-3 and 1953-4 came Coronation Week, and the football club obtained permission from the Welsh F.A. to hold a knock-out competition out of season as part of the local festivities. The Football Association imposed the condition that the local Coronation organizers must approve the football club's plans. After an exchange of letters the Coronation committee did approve. A characteristically reciprocal agreement was entered into. The football club agreed that the profits, not then expected to be large, should be devoted to the general Coronation fund or the losses met by it. In return the parish council, who were controlling the Coronation committee, would provide help during the matches at the gate and in other necessary tasks. The competition was successfully held. Matches were played each evening of Coronation Week, and the final tie played off on the Saturday after the Coronation itself. It was in fact the only successful part of the celebrations in that week. The rest were ruined by the weather.

The Coronation cup final was won by one of the two Pentrediwaith teams entered, but only after some unfortunate incidents which had the immediate sequel that the other finalists left the field and the village some twenty minutes before the end of the game. The ultimate sequel was that the visiting team were rebuked after a local F.A. inquiry and a player was suspended. The following paraphrased report from a local newspaper gives the facts as stated by both sides. The visiting team's allegation that Pentre broke the rules of the competition is, I believe, true, and they had some grounds for complaint if no excuse for their own behaviour.

Team walks off in Coronation Football Final

There was a sensational ending to the final of the Pentrediwaith football knock-out competition on Saturday, when Pentrediwaith 'A' met a Shropshire team. Twenty minutes before full-time, and after an incident in the goal mouth, the visiting side left the field.

It was stated on behalf of the home team that twenty minutes from time, when Pentrediwaith were leading 3—2, the referee awarded a penalty against their opponents for an infringement in the penalty area and at the same time ordered the opposing goalkeeper off the field for—allegedly —striking a Pentrediwaith forward. It is alleged that the visiting team left the field rather than accept the referee's decision.

Their secretary alleges that Pentrediwaith 'A' included in their team four players who had played earlier in the week against his team for the Pentre 'B' team in the same competition. He alleges that when his side strongly objected, they were told that if the four players were not allowed to play there would be no match. Rather than disappoint the large crowd present, which included a fair representation of their own supporters, they agreed to play.

After about 22 minutes in the second half, the secretary says, the goalkeeper was fouled and the referee sounded his whistle for a free kick. The goalkeeper, however, got hold of an opposing forward, whereupon the referee appeared to order the goalkeeper off the field. There was some delay and the referee then indicated a penalty. There was some argument and further delay, and quite a number of spectators were on the field of play when the visiting team left the field, says the secretary.

While he says that his team should not have left the field, he states he is submitting a report of the incidents to the Welsh F.A. and to the local branch of the F.A. with a copy to Pentrediwaith. His complaint is against the organisers of the competition.

Pentre villagers were unanimous in blaming the visitors for what had occurred, and hostility between the villages still survives. On one occasion later in 1953 a group of Pentredi-waith young men were driven from a public house in Bigtown by youths from the other village.

I did not count the number of people present at the disputed match but the gate-money received was nearly £15, and the entrance charge was a shilling. The visitors brought their own supporters with them. This was the largest gate for any Pentredi-waith football match I know of with the single exception of a charity match some years ago when Billy Meredith ceremonially kicked off. The gate on that occasion was nearly £30. The gates received at the other matches during Coronation Week were also good, if not as superlative as for the final, and out of a total income of £48 for the week there was a clear profit of £19. The question of the disposal of this sum soon shattered any hopes of future unanimity of village support for the football club.

Before this issue came up for discussion the annual general meeting already referred to was held and the new committee elected. What to do with the money was almost the first decision we had to make when we first met as a committee; it was preceded only by a revival of the discussion whether the team was to aim at heading the League with outsiders or struggle along with local talent. This discussion had a greater significance than I realized at the time. It was as the secretary, Charley (12), later pointed out, a personal attack on his own position.

The committee then began to discuss the disposal of the £19 profit made by its predecessors in the Coronation competi-tion. I (4) had been told previously, as had the bank clerk chairman (1), that the disposal of these funds was not within the football committee's powers, the money having been promised to the Parish Council Coronation Fund. But when we both mentioned this the secretary (12) denied it was so. In view of the secretary's denial the committee decided to divide the money: three guineas were to be given to the Corona-tion fund, three guineas to the village hall where the meeting was being held and where the football committee always met, and three guineas to the British Legion Benevolent Fund;

the rest was to be put at the disposal of three trustees to administer for the benefit of village charities.

There were heated arguments as to whether the Coronation
committee and the Institute should have any money at all.
These arguments were in each case first put by the English
miner (7), although they did not represent his own personal
views only but also reflected the animosity felt by many villagers towards the parish council, the Coronation committee
and the Institute.

This meeting, like all Pentrediwaith committee meetings,
was supposed to be held in secret. Nevertheless, the next day
these decisions were known and discussed throughout the
village. The chairman of the parish council was particularly
angry at the turn of events. He actually produced Charley's
(12) letter promising the money to the Coronation committee,
and he wrote to the Football Association protesting. It was
also known in the village who had taken which side in the
committee's discussions and the English miner (7) was very
unpopular for trying to prevent any of the money going to the
Coronation committee. The code of reciprocity was invoked:
his wife and child had attended the village Coronation Tea,
and yet he wanted to spite the committee that had organized it.

Since the secretaryship of the supporters' club and of the
Coronation committee (and later of the Carnival committee)
was held by the same woman, the argument was put during
the football committee's discussion that the money must go
to the Coronation committee lest all the women be offended
and the financial aid of the supporters be lost. This argument
was repeated in the village and helped to arouse the antagonism of the women to the football committee. The idea of being
thus lightly bought and sold did not appeal to them.

Charley (12) countered these attacks by saying that the
parish council had not fulfilled their part of the bargain since
no one from that body or from the Coronation committee had
come to help on the gate as had been promised. This was
denied on the grounds that the manager of the Co-operative (2)
had been on the gate twice and, although he was chairman of
the supporters and a football club member, he was also on the
Coronation committee. A more general point, and one which
met with more sympathy in the village, was that even if the

football club was in the wrong it was not right for the parish
council chairman to take the quarrel outside the village by
writing to the F.A. Indeed, for a very brief period this incident
succeeded in uniting the football committee in opposition to
the parish council chairman and his supporters.

While this controversy was at its height in the village,
printed notices appeared in all the shops advertising a sacred
concert to be given by a prize (brass) band on the Sunday
preceding the Royal National Eisteddfod. This is a biennial
event held in Pentrediwaith whenever the Royal National
Eisteddfod is held in North Wales. In 1953, however, there
was a departure from precedent and the posters were marked:
'In aid of the Football Players' Equipment Fund'. As this fund
had never before been heard of, this started more talk in the
village, not least by members of the football committee who
shared in the general ignorance of what this was all about.

It was in this atmosphere of indignation about the Coronation money and doubt about the sacred concert that the new
football committee met for the second time. The first item
on its agenda was the appointment of trustees to administer
the residue of the Coronation Competition funds. (This, of
course, arose out of the decision of the previous meeting to
distribute the fund to certain named charities and devote the
residue to general village charity.) The English miner raised
the general question again in the light of his discovery that
the parish council chairman had in his possession a letter from
the football secretary (12) promising the profits to the Coronation fund. Members blamed the previous committee for not
having handed the money over as soon as they had settled
their expense accounts. It was finally decided to reverse the
previous decision. All the money was now to be given to the
treasurer of the Coronation committee with apologies for
the delay and misunderstanding.

Some days after this meeting the chairman of the parish
council and Charley (12), secretary of the football club, made
up their differences. They agreed that the fault was with neither
of them but was due to the slackness of the village bank manager who had been so slow in compiling the Coronation fund
accounts. The final report on the Coronation committee's
work sent to the local paper a fortnight later included the

following paragraph in which the unity of Pentrediwaith was preserved in the eyes of the outside world:

Special thanks are due to the local Football Club and their energetic Secretary in organizing a knock-out medal competition which brought in over £19.

Thus ended the first major dispute in which the football club was involved in 1953-4. The second dispute started, however, even before the first had finished. At the same meeting of the football committee which reversed its previous decision on the Coronation fund, the question of the sacred concert was raised. The first move in this was made by Humphrey Biggs (6), who (like the principal woman agitator in the matter of the Coronation funds) had a long standing quarrel with Charley (12). He said he had been told by a member of the Committee of the Welsh Football Association who, on a visit to the village, had happened to have tea in the café and hence had seen the poster, that the sacred concert would be against the rules of the Welsh F.A. In any case, Biggs asked: 'Who is running it?'

It appeared afterwards that the Football Association Committee member was fictitious. Like the minister at the parish meeting who threw the onus for his own views upon a former Member of Parliament, Biggs was using the F.A. member to shoulder some of the responsibility for Biggs's own views. I discovered afterwards that no one, with the exception of myself, had been deceived by Biggs's ruse, even at the time.

Charley (12) replied to Biggs's (6) question. He said that he was running the concert himself, with the aid of the football club treasurer, Timothy (3). Normally it was a British Legion affair but, this being August Bank Holiday Week, all the British Legion 'nobs' would be away. For this reason the British Legion had refused to sponsor it, and so he (Charley) was going to run it and give the money to the football club. He had not put 'Football Club' on the posters because it was a Sunday Sacred Concert,[1] and 'it didn't look nice to have a concert for the football on Sunday'. He could not have consulted the

[1] When the concert came off the 'sacredness' was not very apparent. There were fourteen items which included only two hymn tunes. Two others were Eisteddfod test-pieces and the remaining ten ordinary light brass-band music.

football committee as he had had to decide in a hurry, so he had formed his own committee consisting of himself and Timothy (3). The football committee decided that they would take no responsibility for the concert. After a warning against tittle-tattle from the chairman the meeting broke up.

When the committee next met, a week later, it was without Charley (12). He sent a letter to the chairman saying he felt bound to resign because of 'criticism inside and outside the committee'. In the intervening week he had had great difficulty in getting accommodation for the bandsmen, as people were refusing to 'help him line his pockets' and this, he felt, was the last straw. Humphrey (6) was elected to take his place despite his protests. I (4) was asked to be assistant secretary, but I refused to accept formal office although I agreed to continue to help with clerical work as I had done for Charley (12). The necessary contact between the old secretary and the new was also made through me as they were not on speaking terms.

Despite all difficulties the concert was duly held and was a success financially and socially. But it had a sequel. The evening before the football season was due to begin with a home match (in September 1953) the members of the football committee worked on the field preparing it for the next day. In the hotel Charley (12) gave a dinner for the players and committee of the previous season. He paid for this with the proceeeds of the sacred concert. He committed two *faux pas* here. First, it was a festive occasion, although a boycott led to eight empty places and uneaten dinners out of the twenty-four ordered. Alcohol was in fact consumed, and songs were in fact sung, but it was not the debauch village gossip later made it out to be. Secondly, the dinner was not held in the inn owned by the president of the football club but in another pub. Later both these things told heavily against the football club, although it was not responsible for either.

Of the 1953-4 committee the vice-chairman, Percy (2), presided at the dinner. He did not partake of the drinks as he is a teetotaller. The treasurer (3) and one of the miners (9), who had both played the previous season, were also there. Two of the 1952-3 committee and myself (4) who happened to have gone to the pub for a drink also attended. There were five of the players present, and three outsiders staying in the hotel were invited. The other two present were Charley (12) himself and the chairman of the football club, Philip (1). The latter was a special case as he lived in the hotel permanently. When controversy later arose about attendance at the dinner, he claimed that he was merely having his usual meal a little late. He was, he said, just eating in the room, not attending the dinner. This did not deter him from playing the piano to accompany the songs.

The team which turned out next day included five of the diners and was defeated by nine goals to one. It had three more local players (eight) than had originally been chosen and two other changes. The season had got off to a bad start.

The following week the committee failed to choose a team at all on Monday for want of players and had to meet again later in the week. One group in the committee, two miner friends of Charley (9 and 10), put the blame for the bad start on Humphrey (6). Villagers who had been amongst the most active in seeking Charley's (12) removal were now agitating for his return. The next week another of the miner group, Edward (25), a friend of Charley's and brother of Edmond (9), agreed to play for the team and then failed to turn up at the bus. He was afterwards found to have played for another village. The first and only person to speak against him in the committee on account of this was his brother Edmond (9).[1]

At this stage Adam (10), leader of the miner group, signed two more players, and Humphrey (6) signed six. Tension was increased between them when one of Adam's new players was not picked to play. The other did play, but it was generally agreed, and even by Adam, that he was no good.

After this weekly disagreements between Adam (10) and the secretary (6) continued until the final explosion a month later. The conflict came to a head when Adam under the agenda item 'Match Report' said abruptly, and as the opening to the discussion: 'I'd like to know who is supposed to choose the team anyway, the committee or the secretary?' The secretary explained that one of the players had let him down at the last moment and he had had to find a replacement. Adam asked why he had asked Dai Evans, a player from a distance, to play. The committee, Adam asserted with justice, had

[1] See Diagram II on p. 118.

chosen Bill Davies as first reserve. It was well known to the committee that the secretary had opposed the choice of Bill Davies, whom he disliked:

Secretary: 'Bill Davies was going to watch a commercial match with Lloyd on Lloyd's motor-bike.'

Adam: 'Nonsense, man! He was waiting at the hall with his boots.'

Secretary: 'Well, I spoke to Lloyd [another reserve] and he said he was going out with Bill. I thought it was Bill Davies he meant. Perhaps it was Bill Jones.'

Adam: 'Well, I'm through. I'm leaving this Committee.'

Secretary: 'Good riddance to you! You've only been a nuisance.'

The English miner (7) calmed Adam (10) down and restrained him from attacking the secretary. The encounter between Humphrey (6) and Lloyd had taken place in front of my house and I gave evidence about the conversation. The chairman, Philip (1), went round the committee one by one, asking each in turn: 'Do you accept the secretary's version?'

Edmond (9), the miner friend of Charley (12), was the first to answer. He was hesitant but would not give the lie direct. He replied, 'yes', and the other five said 'yes' in turn; only Adam held out, saying: 'No, I'm through!' Bill Davies was fetched from the billiard room nearby and questioned. He confirmed part of the secretary's story. Once more Adam was asked if he accepted the secretary's story. 'No', he said again. No amount of persuasion would make him stay and off he went. Another miner, Edgar (11), brother to William (8) and the team captain, Lance, never attended the committee again after that evening. Although he did not come to the committee to give his views, he was said, like Adam, to think the secretary was too domineering about the team. The committee was now down to its hard core, and it remained in this state for most of 1953.

When Adam had gone, the English miner (7) explained that he worked with Adam and Adam's resignation was, in his opinion, the result of longstanding grievances. The English miner also proposed a resolution that the secretary should have discretion to get whom ever he could to play, once he had exhausted the list of players and reserves chosen by the committee. This same English miner also suggested in private that Edmond (9), another miner, would be the next to go. As Diagram II on p. 118 shows, this prophesy was fulfilled, over two months later. Eventually the chairman (1) also withdrew, and the English miner (7) himself left the district. By mid-December 1953 there was an effective committee of three, the secretary (6), the treasurer (3) and the Co-operative Stores assistant (5).

On a visit I paid to Pentre in late January 1954 I found that the committee had been reinforced by the father and one of the brothers of the secretary. An attempt to get the 1952-3 season's committee to come back had failed. The football club was run informally by the three committee members who remained. Gates continued to diminish and, although village interest still ran high, village support was negligible.

Disputes do not long remain unresolved within the football club. For since the common interest in keeping football going is not sufficient, the committee splits and members resign. But while disputes in committee are solved by the resignation, or a less dramatic falling-off in attendance, of dissident members, the argument continues in the village. Eventually, as had happened by the beginning of 1954, an opposition to the football club grows up. There was a large number of men who would have nothing to do with the football club, and some who went even further and worked against it. The club's posters were torn from trees and players left at short notice to play elsewhere. There was a move, to be described below, to cut off sources of financial aid from the club. A parallel opposition was built up in the women's supporters' club. On a visit to Pentre in September 1954 when the football club had ceased to operate, I learned that although the supporters still had £25 in the bank, they were refusing to let the football committee have it even to pay their outstanding debts.

It seems to me that this sort of development is characteristic in the history of Pentre institutions and, I suspect, of that of similar villages. Efforts are made to avoid conflict, but once a breach is made patent, it spreads through the village. The face-to-face nature of social contacts, and the multiplicity of ties which close residence in an 'isolated' unit brings about, makes this spread inevitable. After a period, which in the case

of the football club was three years from the original difference
over policy, the village becomes so divided that the particular
activity cannot continue. In this case the activity perished
altogether and was replaced by a carnival. At the 1954 carnival which I attended there were significant absences, both
from participation and from the organizing committee, which
indicated that this activity had also already collected its
enemies. Even brief conversations with villagers showed that
it was in process of collecting more. There were also, as we have
seen, indications that the same fate had overtaken previous
activities. Once this process of losing support begins—and
it is of course inherent at the beginning of any activity which
replaces an old one—it is cumulative. Those who remain loyal
to the football, for example, provide a nucleus of resentment
to the carnival. As the opposition grows within the village, the
activity is less likely to succeed in its aims. Thus, as the football committee grew defeatist in outlook and dwindled in
numbers, it was less and less likely to field a winning team.
Pentrediwaith's name appeared weekly at the bottom of the
League table. This increased village hostility to the club
committee and made the committee less efficient.

The carnival, like the football, is also reported in the local
newspaper and has prestige value as a symbol of the village
to the outside world. When, if my predictions are correct, it
ceases to be an efficient symbol, the progress towards its inevitable downfall will be hastened.

Although conflict bedevilled the internal affairs of the football club, efforts were made to avoid it, and in this attempt
strangers played their own familiar role. The English miner (7)
introduced the actual resolutions most likely to split the committee internally, or to isolate it from other villagers. When
conflict did break out, it was he (7) or I (4) who made the
conciliatory moves. Similarly, when Charley (12) and the
chairman of the parish council settled their differences it was
the bank manager, an 'outsider' by class and place of birth,
who was finally given the blame. The chairmen of the football
club in the three seasons I have considered were all Welsh and
Nonconformist, but nevertheless a little removed in outlook
from the committee they led. In the first two seasons the chairmen were employers, although they worked alongside their

men. In season 1953-4, the chairman was a bank clerk who, although he had played for the club and was a Welsh-speaking Chapel-goer, came from elsewhere. During this season the chair was taken in his absence by the English-speaking Co-operative Stores manager or by myself.

Although the differences of opinion which arose were on issues which were real, the individuals who clashed, Charley and Humphrey, Humphrey and Adam, Charley and Tom, were in fact motivated by loyalties and dislikes forged outside the committee or the club. In the case of the football club, conflict triumphed over cohesion, for although the football team symbolized village unity against the outside world, the organization of football was a sectional interest of the men. Amongst the men only a small group were active, although many were interested. There was insufficient external pressure to make them carry on despite their differences.

CARNIVAL AT PENTREDIWAITH

The history of the 1953 carnival in the village went on simultaneously with that of the football club just related but, in contrast to it, was not confined to the men. But although the major conflict was between the organized group of men and the organized group of women, men and women were united not only by other ties external to the carnival situation, but also by their joint acceptance of a limited objective. Their attitude can be summarized by saying that they were united in a desire to make the carnival a financial success, and divided on the question of what to do with the money they hoped to make. Both their unity and their division were reinforced, as are all social relations in Pentrediwaith, by ties of loyalty and dislike carried over from other and seemingly irrelevant situations. The conflicts were partially concealed, and their bitterness mitigated, by forcing strangers to the group into positions of leadership where they had to take the blame for unpopular decisions.

Pentrediwaith Carnival was conceived after the Football Supporters' Club dance which formed part of the Coronation festivities. Coronation 'Queens' were much discussed in the national and local press in the early months of 1953, and at this dance a 'Coronation Football Queen' was chosen and invested with a sash. The secretary of the supporters' club, Betty (14), and the then football club secretary, Charley (12), decided to organize a carnival later in the year at which the chosen 'Queen' could be 'crowned'.[1] They did not, of course, just think of this idea *in vacuo*. Apart from the stirring events at Westminster, there is an annual carnival and 'crowning' in the local market town. In the next village down the valley the annual flower show is accompanied by the crowning of the 'Rose Queen', who is taken by lorry in procession from her village to Pentre and back. Furthermore, the composition of elaborately decorated tableaux on lorries and the making of fancy dress are popular pastimes in this part of Britain. Some Pentre women are particularly expert and compete in contests for the prettiest or funniest fancy dress at many local shows, either in person or through their children.

After the dance the supporters' club devoted itself to preparations for the carnival. I have already mentioned that in 1953 this club was an all women's organization headed by a male chairman, Percy (2). He is in a very real sense outside the group he leads. We have already seen how the football committee is limited in the class from which it draws its membership because of the physical work and duties involved. The supporters' club is united into an abiding interest-group because its members work together in another way. During the preparations for the 1953 carnival, for example, the women concerned met together several times a week as a sewing-group preparing dresses for the 'Queen' and her retinue, the chairman being naturally excluded. Moreover, other village women known to have an interest in this sort of work were drawn in, including some who were openly hostile to the football club. These sewing-group meetings gave the women an opportunity for discussion and argument that was not paralleled in any male institution. Consequently the women were sometimes able to reach unanimity in their attitude to certain matters before they had ever been discussed in open committee. Other conflicts were resolved during the discussions of this informal work group and never came into the open at all.

The supporters' club committee and the extra women who

[1] Numbers in brackets after names refer to Diagram III on p. 136.

were interested in the sewing preparations invited the football
club committee to join with them in organizing the carnival.
They also invited a few men to join in order to carry out
specific tasks. One of these was a Lancashire man, Mr.
Higgins (26), who kept a pet shop in the village and with his
wife ran a kennels nearby. He was invited to organize a dog
show. Another was Rhys (21), who had once been a footballer
for the village but had been dropped from the team. Charley
(12) and Adam (10) remained on the carnival committee
after they had broken with football. Edward (25) continued to
attend even after he had stopped playing for Pentre and started
to play regularly for an English village. Other members of the
football committee disapproved of the carnival and would have
nothing to do with its organization.

I (4) typed the original invitations to join this committee
at Charley's (12) request before he resigned the secretaryship
of the football club. I still possess the original copy in his
handwriting. It reads:

Pentrediwaith F.C.

Carnival Committee

Dear Sir,
        You have been selected a member of the above
Committee. Kindly attend at the Hall on _____ at
7.30 p.m.

Charles _____

Hon. Sec.

I was not present at the first meeting of the carnival committee, which took place just after Charley's (12) resignation from
the football club. This meeting took some decisions which
afterwards assumed great significance. One of these was to
accept Charley's offer to draft the posters, the programme, and
letters of appeal for funds. Charley was also asked to notify
co-opted members of the football club and others of the next
meeting. He had the letters of appeal typed by an English
retired lady living in the village, instead of by me who had
previously done his typing for him. Although no one realized
the significance of this at the time, there was no reference to
the football club either in these letters or in the note which I
and other co-opted members received asking us to attend the

K

carnival committee's second meeting. This was unheaded and read:

Dear Sir,

You are requested to attend a Carnival Committee on Tue. next August 25th 1953 at 7.30 at the hall.

It was signed with Charley's (12) initials. Neither the posters nor the programme which Charley drafted made any reference to the football club.

The committee met and made simple decisions covering the next two weeks; and the women worked and planned dresses and decorations outside the committee. The first signs that there was going to be open conflict in the relations of the football club and the carnival committee did not appear in the latter's proceedings, but in village gossip and at the football committee. Village gossip about a week before the carnival was due to be held was still concerned with the fateful sacred concert and the players' supper at the hotel. There was much to discuss, for not only had the money from a sacred concert been spent on beer, but also there had not been, nor could there be, any balance sheet. The reasons for the lack of published accounts were, first, that the concert had not been sanctioned by the Football Association and, secondly, that the entertainment had taken all the profit and there was none left to spend on equipment. It will be remembered that the concert was held in aid of the 'Football Players' Equipment Fund'. Because of these facts feelings against the football club committee ran high, although it was well known that the existing body had specifically dissociated itself from the concert and the dinner.[1]

In this atmosphere the football committee[2] held its weekly meeting, and at it a miner friend (9) of Charley's (12) asked, after the main discussion was over, if the committee realized that the money from the carnival was not to go to the football club at all but to the carnival committee for next year. He said, when asked, that Charley had told him that the carnival committee had decided this. I (4) said that it had not, in my

[1] In the same way at a general meeting of the supporters' club, the football committee was attacked for opinions expressed by a former committee member three seasons previously.

[2] See Diagram II, p. 118.

knowledge, and Percy (2) said that he was chairman of the carnival committee, which was really just the supporters' committee and, as far as he was concerned, the money was for the football club. In the same week I was told that the question of where the profit was to go was receiving daily discussion in the women's sewing group which was then working every afternoon.

Once the question had come into the open, there followed in the next fortnight two meetings of the carnival committee with a highly successful carnival in between. A week after the last of these meetings the football supporters' club held their annual general meeting—which should in fact have been held before the football season, but had been delayed because of the carnival. These three meetings and the carnival showed very clearly the division of interests between men and women in Pentrediwaith. They also provided the clearest example of the role of strangers in this society.

On the afternoon of the first of these committees, the last formal meeting before the carnival itself, the sewing-group met as usual and discussed the question of not giving any profit they made on the carnival to the supporters' club for football. The supporters' treasurer, Jane (15), told me on her return from this session that she was determined to raise the matter at the committee meeting that evening. The committee met in the main room of the hall with twenty-one people present.[1] At a table in front of the stage, but on the same level as the rest of the committee, sat the chairman, Percy (2), flanked on either side by the treasurer, Jane (15), and secretary, Betty (14), of the supporters' club who were, of course, also treasurer and secretary of the carnival committee. Betty (14), the secretary, was a woman from the oldest part of the village on the hill beside the church; she had also been secretary of the Coronation committee; she was Welsh-born but English-speaking. The treasurer, Jane (15), was Welsh-speaking, Chapel and the wife of a local builder, Tom, who was the founder-chairman of the football club. At this committee meeting, as the diagram shows, members did not sit at random; they were grouped as kin, as cliques and as voting blocs of men against women, women against men. The one man who voted

[1] See Diagram III on p. 136.

Diagram III

FIRST CARNIVAL COMMITTEE

Secretary	Chairman	Treasurer
(14) Betty	(2) Percy	(15) Jane
O	Δ	O

Δ (8) William

Δ (11) Edgar

O (16) Mrs Morgan

Δ (10) Adam

O (17) Mrs Chairman

O (18) Mrs Price   Δ (27) Ian

O (19) Mrs Morgan   Δ (3) Timothy

(20) Mair   (21) Rhys   (12) Charley   (4) Myself
O   Δ   Δ   Δ

O (22)   Δ (26) Mr Higgins

O (23)   Δ (25) Edward

O (24)   Not present but active
                    O (28) Mrs Green

Carnival Committee Members' Inter-relationships

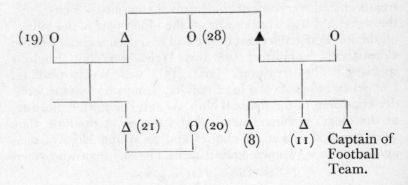

with the women and two other dissident men are (21), (12) and (25) in the diagram and, as can be seen, they are on the fringe of the men's group. All the committee members were villagers in the territorial sense except myself (4) and Mr. Higgins (26); (8) and (11) were born in Pentre but lived in the next village.

Although they did not all act in this situation as kin, many members were closely related: (2) and (17) were husband and wife; (27) was the son of (15) and (3) was courting (15)'s daughter; I (4) lived at (15)'s house; the largest group linked by kinship were (19), (20), (21) and (28), and they acted and voted as a group; (8) and (11) were also related to these but acted independently (their relationship is shown below the main diagram); (19), (20) and (21) lived together on the main street of the village, and it was in a room of theirs that the sewing-group met. In addition (28) was the next-door neighbour, collaborator in handicrafts and friend of (18); (23) was actually the daughter of (18), but they had quarrelled very seriously and were not on speaking terms; (22), (23) and (24) were close friends and attended football matches together; they did not share the sewing interests of the other women and were, in fact, very much younger than any of the others; (23) was also brother's daughter to (10). All the women except (22) were married; the three men who were not were either engaged or 'courting strong'; (12) and (25) were both miners in 1953, having been friends previously and having entered the mines when a bakery business in which they were partners failed; (10), (11) and (8) were members of what I have called the 'miners' group' of the football committee.[1]

When this committee met there was some general discussion; then Mrs. Morgan (19) raised the question of the disposal of the surplus carnival funds. She said she had done a lot of work for it and was raffling a chair to raise money. She did not see why the football club should take all the money and the carnival have to start from scratch again the following year. She would not have helped to raise money just for the football

---

[1] There were more distant relationships involved in this committee, though they were never mentioned in the discussion of events. I learned of them only through specific enquiries and in general discussion on the theme: 'All Pentre villagers are related.'

club to waste. She had not realized it was in aid of the football. She formally proposed that a proportion of the profits be put aside for the carnival next year. When the chairman (2) called for discussion on this proposition, saying that he personally was opposed to it, Mrs. Morgan (19) immediately withdrew her proposition, but the discussion continued. This happens frequently in Pentrediwaith: if a local proposer makes a suggestion he withdraws it as soon as it shows signs of raising controversy.

Most of the men present, including myself (4) and Charley (12), spoke against this plan, but Rhys Morgan (21) supported his mother (19). He said the football club would only waste the money. He had come on the committee to help at the carnival, not to help the football club. Nothing had been said on the programme or the posters about football. I was told afterwards that this branch of the Morgan family had quarrelled with the football club, two or three years previously, when after only one game Rhys (21) had been dropped from the team.

After a great deal more discussion, in which most took part and the same points were reiterated, Mr. Higgins (26), an outsider to the village, intervened with great vigour. He pointed out that the football supporters' club had provided the initial finance and would stand the loss if there was one. It would be positively illegal for them not to get the profit. He proposed: 'That all the profits go to the Football Supporters' Club.' This motion was put, and carried after a show of hands, by 11 votes to 9. All the men except Rhys voted for this motion. The only women who did were the chairman's wife (17) and another (and unrelated) Mrs. Morgan (16) who had not, I was told later, been attending the sewing-group. Both the secretary (14) and the treasurer (15) of the supporters voted against their organization receiving the money. This matter, it appeared at the time, being settled, the committee proceeded with its business. This was actually another dispute, but this time amongst the women only. It was a question as to which village children should attend the 'Carnival Queen'. The argument was carried on by the women who were anxious for this honour for their own children or grandchildren.

The women of the sewing-group who presented so united a

front at the committee did not accept defeat, and the argument continued over tea and sewing for the next two days. Outside the committee meetings the women were not so united; (22), (23) and (24) insisted that the decision was right, and so did the treasurer of the supporters (15) although she had voted against it. The other women said that (22), (23) and (24) had not done any of the sewing, so had no right to an opinion.

As for the men, the women said that none of them had done anything except Charley (12). This was admitted by the men, but they countered with the true observation that although in the nature of things most of the preparation had been done by women, on the day itself the stalls and much of the adminis-tration would be run by men. Mair (20), wife of Rhys (21), announced that, whatever happened, the proceeds of the raffle for a chair, which she was conducting, were not going to go to the football.

But all the dissidents were united in support of Mrs. Green's (28) view that the whole business was the fault of that Mr. Higgins (26), a 'stranger', who had interfered in Pentre affairs. 'All strangers', she said, 'ought to be shot!' And on that note the carnival itself was held.

A detailed account of the carnival is not necessary here. It is enough to note that, despite false starts and minor catas-trophes, the carnival was held and enjoyed. Profits from raffles and competitions and the original football dance, together with the profits of the carnival and the carnival dance, came to nearly £60. The gross receipts were over £80. The unex-pected size of the profits intensified the rivalry of the claimants, but things remained formally quiet until ten days later, when the winding-up meeting of the carnival committee was held. Only fourteen of the original members attended this. A plan of the seating at the start of the meeting is on page 140.

The meeting started with Percy (2) as usual in the chair. He had, however, to leave early because of another engagement. Other affairs had occupied the village since the carnival and Percy did not, he said later, think that further argument about the disposal of the profits would take place that evening. Before he left the tone of the discussion was set. It began in dis-cord. Betty (14) said she had forgotten to bring the minutes of the last meeting. When one of the men offered to fetch them she amended this; she had forgotten to write them. The important decision of the previous meeting was thus not recorded in writing. The chairman (2) gave a resumé from memory of what had taken place at the meeting. He referred to the great success of the carnival and went on to single out for praise the secretary (14) and Charley (12). This brought immediate protest from Mrs. Price (18), who instead praised Mrs.

Diagram IV

WINDING-UP MEETING OF CARNIVAL

Secretary	Chairman	Treasurer
(14) Betty	(2) Percy	(15) Jane
O	Δ	O

(17)	(19)	(18)	(26)
Mrs Chairman	Mrs Morgan	Mrs Price	Mr Higgins
O	O	O	Δ

(25)	(12)	(4)	(3)
Edward	Charley	Myself	Timothy
Δ	Δ	Δ	Δ

(23)	(22)	(24)
O	O	O

Morgan (19) who had let the sewing-group use her room, another villager who had lent a lorry, and the chairman's enemy (not hitherto mentioned) who had lent his house and his services for making paper-flowers.[1] The chairman apologized for his omissions and then tried to go, but he was 'persuaded' to stay and answer criticisms on his running of the children's sports at the carnival. They too were made by Mrs. Price (18). This matter settled, Percy (2) announced that there was now only routine business of the supporters' club left and he went off to a rehearsal of his drama group. I myself was moved into the chair.

The question of who was to take the raffle tickets round the field the following Saturday was soon settled, and I asked for

[1] This man had once been a member of Percy's (2) 'Church' drama group. He had quarrelled with Percy and formed his own 'Chapel' drama group.

'Any Other Business'. I did not expect any and was ready to close the meeting. But Charley (12) said there was just one point; he was not clear where the profit from the carnival was to go. To clarify things he wanted to put a motion to delete the previous committee's minute and substitute: 'That the money be divided fifty-fifty between the Football Supporters' and a Carnival Fund.'[1] He said that, after all, it had not been specified on the posters or appeals for funds that the carnival was connected with the football. Mr. Higgins (26), the Lancashire man who had suffered much criticism for his previous stand on behalf of football and the letter of the law, put an amendment to Charley's motion: 'That £25 be given to the Football Supporters' and the rest kept by the Carnival'. No one would second either of these proposals and argument continued. The secretary, Betty (14), said that the supporters' had not financed the carnival at all. The treasurer (15) corrected her privately on this at the officers' table, occupied at the time only by myself (4) and these two. The correction was not audible to the main part of the committee, nor would the treasurer repeat it when I gave her an opening. She explained next day in conversation that the supporters had in fact financed the carnival to the extent of £11. She had not stated this openly in the committee because, as she said: 'I hope to live in the village all my life and I don't want to be at odds with my neighbours. I worked with the other women sewing and I know what they think about it.'

After more discussion in the committee, Mr. Higgins (26) who, it will be remembered, had put an almost directly opposite motion ten days before, proposed that £30 be given to the carnival fund and that two trustees and a treasurer be appointed to administer this fund. His proposal was passed, by show of hands, unanimously and with acclamation. Betty (14), the secretary, and Mrs. Price (18) were appointed trustees and Mrs. Morgan (19) was made treasurer. I (4) adjourned the meeting amidst general affability and self-approbation. Mrs. Morgan (19) and the supporters' treasurer

---

[1] Although the official name is the Football Supporters' Club, it is always referred to simply as 'The Supporters'. There were some women who argued that, this being so, they could support anything they wanted, but this argument was not taken very seriously even by the anti-football faction within the club.

(15) both said after the meeting that in future the carnival committee and the supporters' would work together.

This general agreement did not long survive the adjournment of the committee, and members were involved in bitter arguments that evening. For example, the treasurer's (15) son, Ian (27), who had not attended this meeting, held that the decision was illegal; his mother (15) accepted this the next day, and said she would refuse to pay the cheque to the new carnival fund treasurer. During the next day every member of the committee that I met was claiming that she at least had not voted, and therefore could not be held responsible for the decisions of others. Discussion continued in the village, but two days later, when Mrs. Morgan (19), the new carnival treasurer, came to collect the cheque she was given it without argument. I gathered in the village that I (4) and, to some extent, Mr. Higgins (26) were being blamed for the whole affair. It was asserted, probably with truth, that the proposal would not have been accepted if Percy (2) had stayed on to chair the meeting until its close.

Thus once more unpopularity incurred by making a decision which divided villagers was passed on to those it would least harm, and whose unpopularity had least effect on normal social relations within the village. In this case, Percy (2) who left early, either by accident or by design, avoided the criticism which, as a villager slightly different from the others, he usually received. His place was taken by Mr. Higgins (26) and myself (4), two complete 'outsiders'. Despite this satisfactory apportionment of blame, it was expected that the controversy would be revived at the annual general meeting, now overdue, of the football supporters' club. This was open to the whole village. The sting had gone out of the argument, however, since the money had been paid over and no one expected that the trustees and the treasurer of the carnival fund would in any circumstances agree to its return.

The annual general meeting of the supporters illustrates well the division of opinion between men and women in Pentrediwaith. This had been clear throughout the controversy and had been exploited by Charley and the Morgans for their own ends. At the general meeting the division was made completely explicit. Diagram V on p. 144 gives the seating plan and attendance at this meeting. Percy (2) did not attend and his place was taken by Philip (1), the chairman of the football club, who had been away from the village on holiday during most of the carnival controversy and during the carnival itself.

Philip (1) opened the meeting by saying what a pleasure it was for him to preside over the supporters. This was especially so, because by their magnificent efforts in running a carnival, they had raised so much money for the football club. He was sorry to have been away and to have missed the carnival. He had heard that £30 of the sum raised was going to a carnival fund. Not, of course, that the football club begrudged the money; but, after all, the football supporters' had put up the original £7 (sic) and the football club would have suffered any loss incurred. Charley (12) 'begged to differ' about this and reiterated his now familiar point that the posters and the letters made no reference to the football club. Jane's (15) son, Ian (27), asked innocently who had drafted the notices. Jane, the supporters' treasurer (15), recalled that the carnival committee and the supporters had at the winding-up meeting of the carnival undertaken to work together in future. This recollection was not entirely accurate, as this undertaking was made only after the meeting had ended. But there were, of course, no minutes to verify or disprove it. Charley (12) and Timothy (3) denied it and Charley (12) appealed to me (4) to support him. On this occasion, however, after the week of sidelong glances which had followed my last intervention as chairman, I kept silent and would not comment one way or the other.

Mrs. Morgan (19), treasurer of the carnival fund, said they did not want to give all the money to the football club to spend, as the club might go out of existence and then they would have nothing to show for their carnival efforts. They were quite willing to hold the carnival next year in aid of the football again if the club still existed. Ian (27), who came to Pentre only on brief visits, said that that was all very well, but the football supporters had started a carnival, and now the situation was reversed. A carnival committee was very generously saying that they might give the football club a donation. It seemed sharp practice to him.

Charley (12) said that he would like to know why, while

Diagram V

ANNUAL GENERAL MEETING OF SUPPORTERS' CLUB

Secretary (14) Betty O	Football Club Chairman (1) Philip △	Treasurer (15) Jane O

(17) Mrs Chairman O	(19) Mrs Morgan O	

(22) O	(24) O	(6) Football Club

	(12) Charley △	(4) Myself △	Secretary Humphrey △

(3)
Football
Club

(27) Ian △	(29) Lloyd △	Treasurer Timothy △

usually the supporters' treasurer (15) signed cheques on her own, the cheque paying £30 to the carnival fund had had to be signed by the chairman (2) as well. It appeared that what in fact had happened was that the bank had required a 'minute' opening the account, as is usual bank practice. This had built up in village rumour to the story given by Charley (12). This part of the discussion was closed when Philip (1) revealed that the football club was having difficulty in raising its usual donations, because the donors who had given to the carnival felt that they had done their bit, and would give no more to the club.[1] At this point in Philip's statement Charley (12),

---

[1] The football club's income by donation from its president, vice-presidents and the brewery companies is between £25 and £30. The carnival raised only £15 by direct donations. In fact, although Philip (1) did not mention it at this stage, the players' dinner by its snub to the publican-president had cost the club his substantial donation.

who was working the night-shift in the pit, had to leave. His departure was the signal for an almost audible relaxation of tension and Philip, amidst murmurs of agreement, put squarely upon Charley's shoulders the blame for the admittedly bad relations between the football club and the majority of villagers. The incidents of the Coronation funds, the players' dinner, and his alleged extravagance in bringing outside players to home matches by taxi, were all mentioned and unanimously condemned.

The 'footballers', however, were not to escape as lightly as that. Once the carnival quarrel had been disposed of by blaming it on Charley, the women had other things to speak of. The supporters' committee members took it in turn to detail the way in which the men failed to carry out, or even recognize, their reciprocal obligations. The cases they cited had in fact happened in previous seasons when other individuals had controlled the football committee. Jane (15), the supporters' treasurer, for example, told how she had asked a certain footballer three seasons previously, although she did not say so at the meeting, to buy a whist drive ticket. He had refused. She continued:

> 'What would you footballers do without the Supporters' Club?' I said.
> 'Huh, what would the Football Supporters' Club do with no one to support?' he said.
> 'Well', I said, 'I always knew you were ignorant, but I didn't realize you were such a fool as that!'

Mrs. Morgan (19) then told how, when she had been on the supporters', she had gone to an away match on the bus with the team. She had had to pay two shillings, whereas the football committee members had travelled free. This had also happened two years previously. (In 1953 football committee members paid their share with the rest.) The secretary (14) then raised the vexed question of the men's attendance at whist drives. Timothy (3), stung, retorted that someone had to pick a team, and if the supporters *would* arrange whist drives on Mondays when the football committee met, what did they expect? Betty replied: 'Fair play for Charley! He always comes, even on Monday.' Humphrey (6), the secretary of the football club, and Timothy (3), its treasurer, promised to be economical in future, and that all the football committee would try and come to whist drives.

This discussion was followed by a rapid election for the supporters' committee. The chairman, Percy (2), and the secretary, Betty (14), were re-elected. The treasurer, Jane (15), resigned on the grounds of ill-health. Aided by Ian (27), her son, she managed to escape the treasurership but not the committee. Mrs. Morgan (19), already treasurer of the carnival, was persuaded to take the post for the supporters as well. This, largely the work of Philip (1), was an astute move,[1] as it not only brought in the group that she controlled, but it also resolved the feud between that group and the football club. In addition, it ensured that if the football survived, the carnival committee would co-operate with the supporters' club, since the officers of both were the same and fear of public opinion would prevent them favouring one club at the expense of the other; (17), (22) and (24) were re-elected in addition to (23) who had deliberately stayed away in the vain hopes of avoiding re-election. Finally, two young unmarried girls, one still at school, were added to the committee. It was explained that, since they always went to home matches because of their interest in the young men, they could be put to good use as raffle-ticket sellers. The elections completed, the meeting adjourned and so ended, at least for the moment, the controversy which surrounded the disposal of the carnival funds.

This account of the formal meetings concerning the carnival finances, and the relations of the carnival to the football supporters' club, gives the framework of the dispute. But the argument was not confined to the handful of villagers who attended these meetings. Nearly everyone in the village knew about it and discussed it. It was for a period almost the only topic of conversation in the pubs and in the shops. It divided households, at least all the families I knew best and visited regularly.

The protagonists of different points of view in the committees and at the meetings were spokesmen for the village. But these spokesmen were affected by many factors entirely unconnected either with the aims of the committees or the proceedings them-

[1] Or would have been if the football club had survived. Since writing this I have learned that it did not.

selves. Decisions were taken and a compromise made after a complicated process of argument inside and outside the committees. The side that people took was determined not by an impartial, objective judgment on the real issues involved, but by their own social position in the community as individuals and as members of particular groups. At the same time the division of interests between men and women dominated the discussions. Thus Charley (12) was motivated by his own relations to the football club, as a result of its dispute with the parish council and also for more profound reasons already discussed. But he had to reconcile this attitude with his position as a man and as a member of the sectional group of miners. It will be remembered that he voted with the men at the first meeting. Jane, the supporters' treasurer (15), had to balance her own position as a woman amongst the other women of the sewing-group against her responsibilities as treasurer. She had the choice of annoying her fellow women, or the men of her own household and of the village.

The men in general were concerned with the continuance of football and ensuring that the club got the money it needed. The women's sewing-group wanted to ensure that they had means to continue with their hobby of making decorations and fancy dress. Their attitude was complicated by previous disagreements with the football club as individuals suffering personal slights, and as a group with interests opposed to those of the men.

At the crucial points in the public discussions, villagers like Mrs. Morgan (19) and Charley (12) made suggestions which precipitated crisis, but they then withdrew into the background and allowed a stranger to come forward and put the formal motions which actually split the committee and village opinion. After the first two committee meetings a stranger was blamed, and although Charley (12) too was blamed in his absence at the third villagers gave little public recognition to their own divisions. Their general verdict was that they could have managed all right, but that strangers *would* interfere and cause trouble.

V

CONCLUSIONS

IN this book I attempt to make a social anthropological analysis of a limited part of our own society. Since that part contains many of the complexities of the whole society there are major difficulties in attempting this analysis, especially in view of the short period I was able to give to the study. These are offset to some extent by the advantages of studying a community with a known history and environment, the basic values of which are readily understood. This has enabled me to dispense with much of the introductory material on ecology and general background which usually prefaces such analyses.

The social sciences are not the only ones which have to deal with complex reality. If I wish to understand the chemistry of living cells I can approach the study by isolating a process in a test-tube, and then stopping it at intervals and examining the equilibrium that has been reached. This equilibrium is, of course, an artificial one which is obtained by intervening and stopping the process from outside. But if I make a series of such analyses at different times from the beginning of the process and vary the external conditions (temperature, for example), a picture of the process as a whole can be built up.

This study of a North Wales village is an attempt to study social processes in an analogous way.[1] For a short period of

[1] It is not of course an original approach. After I had written the above, I re-read Gluckman, M., 'Social Situation in Modern Zululand', *Bantu Studies*, xiv (1940), 1 and 2, where, except for the biochemical analogy, I found the problem stated in almost identical terms (p. 29): 'It is these conflicts within the Zululand structure which will lead to its future developments, and by clearly defining them in my analysis of the temporary equilibrium, I hope to relate my cross-section study to my study of change. Therefore, I suggest that in order to study social change in South Africa the sociologist must analyse the equilibrium of the Black-White community at different times and show how successive equilibria are related to one another.'

time I lived in a small village and observed its life. I have now
presented description, analysis, and interpretation of some of
the facts I observed in that place and at that time. But I
know them to be true only of Pentrediwaith and of a single
year. To 'set up the experiment' some indication of the external environment and of its history had also to be given.
I have then been concerned with some aspects of the social
life of a village. Into the social field of this village intruded
factors from the wider social systems of county and nation.
The field was affected also by factors arising out of the lives of
the villagers in a narrower sphere, their households and their
families. It was a village made up of individuals, families and
groups; and it was part of Wales.

At the beginning of the book therefore I tried to describe how
the village had come to be as it was, and how it was related
to other parts of Britain and to Wales. It seemed to me that
some knowledge of the history of the village itself and of the
country of which it forms a part was an essential first stage for
a study of this kind.

The two groups in Pentrediwaith which I have called
'Outsiders' and 'Pentre People' are the outcome of developments in Wales similar to the Irish Catholic peasantry and
English Protestant landowner division in Ireland.[1] The
Anglican, English-speaking landowners once stood openly
opposed in outlook and economic interest to their Welsh Nonconformist tenants and labourers. They may still do so in
some parts of Wales. But in Pentrediwaith, as I have tried to
show, the situation is more complex. The basic clash of economic interests now occurs outside the village altogether.
English gentry as such no longer retain power or importance
in the village, but English industrial culture is now regarded
as a threat. The criteria of 'English-speaking' and 'Church-
membership' no longer divide merely the main economic
classes but also form the basis of less fundamental divisions
within the village. These attributes, which are associated
with class differences in Wales as a whole and which have
been so important in Welsh history, play a different role
inside the village. For, as I have described, a substantial num-

[1] See Arensberg and Kimball, p. 29; Pomfret, J., *The Struggle for Land
in Ireland*, 1800-1923, Princeton, 1930.

L

ber of ordinary wage-earning villagers do not, in fact, normally speak Welsh or attend Chapel. Husband and wife may prefer to speak different languages and profess allegiance to different denominations. Next-door neighbours and friends may be divided in their membership of Church and Chapel. Only in specific social contexts do these differences become significant.

Remnants of the original class antagonism between English landlord and Welsh tenant persist in modern Pentrediwaith. The influence of economic class is most clearly shown in the membership of local government institutions, and in the official relations of Pentrediwaith councillors and magistrates with similar bodies outside the village and the valley. I have tried to show (in Chapter III) how economic class divisions are accurately reflected in the election of parish councillors and others, and in their subsequent behaviour. But even in these institutions there is not an uncomplicated opposition of economic interests. The relations between the wage-earners, who form the class from which parish councillors are drawn, and the salaried and self-employed, who make up the County Council and the Magistrates' Bench, are complicated by a factor of 'scale'. Parish councillors are men with local interests and knowledge. They are deeply and intensively involved in social activities but in a very narrow sphere. They do not concern themselves with, or even show curiosity about, the affairs of even neighbouring villages in the valley. The 'magisterial' or 'vice-presidential' class participate in the social life of many villages both inside and outside the valley. They are not, however, deeply involved in any single village.

The intensely local preoccupations of the parish councillors have a more general effect on their behaviour, as a body, in relation to other parish councils in the county. As we have seen, the Parish Councils Association of the county meets alternately in the rural west and industrial east. In the minds of the people of the county, Welshness is connected with the west of the county and rural culture, and an English outlook is linked with residence in the industrial east. This is broadly a correct picture, but there are significant exceptions. One is the village of Pentreglo, which we found to be more influenced in its external relations with other parishes by its industrial nature than by its Welshness. In their attitude both to English-speaking

CONCLUSIONS   151

industrial areas and to Welsh-speaking Pentreglo, Pentre villagers identified themselves with the rural parts of the county.
In their daily life and work the men of Pentrediwaith are
becoming more and more involved in the English-speaking
industrial economy surrounding Tonmawr.

This uneasy contradiction between Pentrediwaith's past as a
small-scale rural community (albeit based on slate-mining
rather than on farming) and its present integration into industrial Britain also affects social relations within the village.
For although most men travel away from the village and work
side by side with men from other places, the women still remain
in Pentrediwaith for both work and recreation. The men's
interests are largely turned towards the problems and amusements of the industrial society outside, while the women remain preoccupied, despite the influence of radio and television,
with the affairs of the village. This difference in outlook of
men and women pervades all social activity and provides a
major division in village social life which cuts across all others.

This state of affairs is, of course, in sharp contrast to the situation in peasant and small-farmer communities where, although
men and women have separate tasks and spheres of activity,
their roles are complementary.[1] In such circumstances men
and women are united by their respective roles in a division
of labour advantageous to both. In Pentrediwaith men and
women only unite, in this context, to condemn the external
circumstances which have forced them apart. Obviously a
division between men and women cannot be absolute. Men
and women marry and set up households. They co-operate
within the home to rear their children, and sometimes they
both contribute to a joint family income. Men are related,
through their wives, affinally and informally to other groups
than their own. Relationships of friendship and hostility in
various alliances between single and related households and
their neighbours enter into the working of village communal
affairs.

Because of Pentrediwaith's place in the wider structure and
culture of Britain, external influences lead to the setting up

[1] See the works of Rees, West, and Arensberg and Kimball, listed in the
Bibliography. See also Loomis and Beegle, *Rural Social Systems*, New York,
1950.

of social activities within the village. Men and women, separately and together, form committees to organize and carry on such activities. Examples are Eisteddfod 'parties', Coronation celebrations, carnivals, and football. Loyalties and enmities forged outside these specific activities are carried over into them, until individuals are forced to make decisions which reveal their personal divided loyalties and may also reveal social divisions in the village. It is in order to save Pentre people themselves from making these critical decisions that strangers are forced into positions of leadership in the village. That these leaders are in fact themselves led is shown by the inconsistency of their attitude on village issues. We saw, for example, how the strangers involved in both the Carnival fund dispute and the dispute over the disposal of the Coronation football profits reversed their own previous opinions at the second discussion. Between the time that I took the chair at a Carnival Supporters' Committee meeting and the time of the Football Supporters' Annual General Meeting, I also experienced the uncomfortable village pressure that caused them to change their views.

Even the employment of strangers in this role and the use of other devices to avoid conflict were not always successful. Consequently, when the desire to continue an activity was not strong enough to override conflicts, groups of villagers resigned from organizing committees. For this reason, it seemed to me, each kind of recreational activity built up, in the course of its existence, opposition to itself as an activity, independently of the personnel currently engaged in it. This was complicated by interpersonal and intergroup 'feuds' amongst its personnel. Some of these 'feuds' arose from the carrying out of the activity; others were carried over from other outside relationships. The football club had in 1953 reached a stage when support was so much weaker than opposition that it could no longer carry on. Conversation with villagers led me to suppose that a similar fate had overtaken other activities in the past.

Recreational activities which bring the village into contact and competition with other villages have another function as well. They serve, as the football club did in the years after the war until 1953, as a symbol of village prestige and unity in the face of the outside world. Their exploits are recorded in the local newspapers and noised abroad by villagers. But the internal divisions to which they give rise decrease their efficiency as symbols. The football club won only two games in the 1953-4 season. The quality of performance of the brass band and the choir also decreased as they began to crumble. This external failure in turn still further weakens the internal position of the activity. A poor performance at a football match or play or eisteddfod spoils the village's reputation. I suspect that this hypothesis, of increasing internal and external failure as conflicts surrounding an activity grow, may be more widely applicable.[1]

We have seen that, in Pentrediwaith, activities are started with practical aims and in emulation of similar activities in neighbouring, and even distant, parts of England and Wales. Many Pentre villagers enjoy playing and watching association football, Britain's national game. Other villagers like to sing or play brass-band instruments or to listen to those who do. At different times in the past villagers attracted to these and other recreational pursuits have combined with others to take part in them. When they form associations of this kind, there are national organizations in which they can take their place and play their part. But since Pentre people feel themselves to be a community, when they combine with fellow-villagers to form a team or 'party' their association becomes more than a convenient arrangement based on the 'accident' of living together. Combining in recreational activities has social value to the villagers because it emphasizes their relationships one to another in a community. This is true of all communities. But it is especially important when the men no longer work together. In this kind of situation recreational activities provide the only system in which they can 'interact' as members of a community.[2]

But these recreational activities often involve competition with other villages and groups. The football team and the brass band take part in contests with those of other villages.

---

[1] The rise and fall of social activities in British communities has often been commented on. See for example the works of Kempe and Whiteley listed in the Bibliography.

[2] See Homans, G., *The Human Group*, for general discussion on the relations of *interaction* and *sentiment*. For particular discussion in a somewhat similar situation to Pentrediwaith, see his discussion of Hilltown in ch. xiii.

The Carnival and Coronation festivities are judged by the general standards of the surrounding countryside. Therefore, in addition to serving as an internal symbol of the villagers' enduring community of interests, these activities become also a symbol of the village's existence as a community in opposition to other communities and the world at large. Thus activities with their own 'practical' ends acquire a symbolic value for the villagers in their external relationships with other villagers. They provide also a medium through which internal village disputes and conflicts find expression. These disputes and conflicts are essentially personal and informal. They arise from the relationships of individual to individual and household to household in a face-to-face society. When an activity is abandoned the conflicts within the village are, temporarily at least, suspended at the same time as the activity they have killed. Thus village unity is emphasized and maintained.

In Pentrediwaith recreational activities are not connected with prosperity or with an institutionalized structure in the village, as they are in some primitive societies.[1] They arise from the meeting of individual interests, where there is no structural arrangement of relations between these individuals, although villagers feel that the village ought to have communal activities. Hence the conflicts which intrude into the activities are between individuals in unformalized relations, and their expression does not end in a return to an ordained pattern of relations. The system is repetitive only in a limited field, and the significant divisions in the society between 'Pentre people' and 'outsiders' remain unaffected. For these last are reflections of national alignments over which Pentre villagers have no control.

In Pentrediwaith conflicts are carried over from one form of recreational activity to another, as from football to carnival. Furthermore, the new conflicts engendered in disputes over football and carnivals may extend back into everyday life and cause further divisions within the village. The degree of success with which villagers continue to co-operate in new activities is a measure of the success with which they are meeting the threat of losing their discrete village identity. But some individuals withdraw in anger or disgust and refuse to

---

[1] Gluckman, M., *Rituals of Rebellion in South East Africa*, The Frazer Lecture 1952, Manchester University Press, 1954.

take any further part in village activity. When this happens only the sanction of public disapproval can bring them back. It is possible (but I cannot verify this) that the lack of success of Pentrediwaith activities may itself be important in that it concentrates the attention of villagers on to recreational activities. This in turn makes such activities the medium through which villagers express their personal rivalries, conflicts and ambitions.

I have tried to show how Pentre people use 'strangers' in this context. This provides one with a point of comparison. In all societies in which opposing groups must continue to live and gain their livelihood side by side there are mechanisms which tend to avoid or diminish conflict between groups. The use of strangers in Pentrediwaith to accept responsibility for decisions which split village opinion is by no means unique. Similar appeals to 'external authority' are structural devices which have often been analysed by social anthropologists. The form is the same although the cultural context may be very different in various places and at different times. The leopard-skin chief amongst the Nuer, the Senussi in Cyrenaica,[1] and the monastic settlements in early Wales[2] all provide examples of 'stranger' groups which played the same role. These were all protected from the consequences of unpopularity by their relations with the spiritual world. Joking-partners amongst the Tonga of Northern Rhodesia are another slightly different instance.[3] The making of decisions by consulting magical oracles or oracles revealing the ancestors' wishes achieves the same result in yet another way.[4]

But in these examples there is a sharp distinction between the practices of Africa and those of Pentrediwaith. The stranger

[1] Evans-Pritchard, E. E., *The Nuer*, Oxford, 1940, and *The Sanusi of Cyrenaica*, Oxford, 1949.

[2] Lloyd, Sir John, *History of Wales from the Earliest Times to the Edwardian Conquest*, vol. 1, London, 1911.

[3] Colson, E., 'Clans and the Joking-Relationship among the Plateau Tonga of Northern Rhodesia', *Kroeber Anthropological Society Papers*, Nos. 8 and 9, California, 1953.

[4] A clear statement of this is made by Professor Fortes, who ends a description of the deciding of a dispute by the elders with this paragraph: 'However, to make the decision conclusive and to save it from rankling it was left to an oracle. A fowl was slaughtered with an invocation to the ancestors and the posture in which it died showed which of the disputants was in the right. No one was surprised when Tinta'alem gained the verdict. Thus the ancestors themselves vouched for the legitimate status of Yidaan biis'. Fortes, M., *The Dynamics of Clanship among the Tallensi*, 1945, p. 70.

in Africa, whether human or spirit, acts through mystical
sanctions to prevent the divisions inherent in a formal structure
from breaking into open conflict. In Pentrediwaith the stranger
has no ritual power or licensed freedom to protect him. He is
merely removed from the informal conflicts which, with his
help, may be resolved without awakening open hostilities.
When such a stranger is also an 'Outsider' his exclusion from
informal social contacts is almost complete. For he not only
lacks kinship ties with 'Pentre People', but is also excluded,
both as a participant and as a subject, from the gossip and
backbiting of the community. He may not join in criticism of
Pentre people, and his own affairs, however scandalous, are
of merely passing interest.[1]

Professor Barnes has written of a modern Norwegian
community:

> Each person in Bremnes belongs to many social groups.
> In particular he is a member of a household, of a hamlet,
> of a ward, and he is a member of the parish of Bremnes.
> At different times and different places membership of one or
> other of these groups is definitive for what he does. He goes
> to the prayer-house with his household, sits at weddings
> with other members of his hamlet, and pays tax according
> to his parish. There are other series of groups which to some
> extent cut across these territorially-based ones, although they
> may themselves be based on territory. Thus, for example,
> a man may belong to a hamlet missionary working-party,
> or to a bull-owning co-operative based on a ward. In formal
> terms these various groups fit one inside the other, each in
> its own series. Thus there are three territorially-defined
> fishermen's associations in the parish. All three belong to
> the provincial fishermen's association, and this in its turn
> forms part of the national association. There may be
> conflicts because of the duties and rights a person has in
> the various groups in any one series, and there may be
> conflicts because of his interests in different series. This is
> true of all societies.[2]

[1] Cf. Colson, *The Makah Indians.*
[2] Barnes, J. A., 'Class and Committees in a Norwegian Island Parish',
Human Relations, vii, 1954, i, pp. 40-41. For a full exposition of this view
see Gluckman, M., 'Political Institutions' in Evans-Pritchard, E. E., *et al.,*
The Institutions of Primitive Society, Blackwell, 1954 (especially p. 77). See
also Gluckman, M., 'Social Situation in Modern Zululand', *Bantu Studies,*
xiv, 1940, 1, 2, p. 27; and Professor Fortes's statement in *Dynamics of*

I have tried in this book to establish the existence of this principle and to analyse in detail its operation in yet another field of social enquiry. I hope that my study emphasizes also one important point which has emerged from other studies. Despite all the cross-cutting divisions, a group such as the Swazi or the Tale people or a Zulu village has symbolic activities which are expressive of its unity. So, too, if a village in Wales is a village it undertakes activities which are village activities. All individuals are expected to join in independently of their relations with one another. If the observations of this study are borne out elsewhere, it seems that we may be able to say that if there are no such activities we have a housing-unit and not a village. Perhaps also my study of recreation in Pentrediwaith emphasizes that some form of 'ceremonial' in the sense of joint symbolic activities is necessary to maintain group loyalty in an acephalous community. This seems to me especially true when the men of the group no longer work together.

Pentrediwaith, despite its position in England and Wales, still remains in some senses isolated and therefore united. In the past villagers worked together, played together and lived together. Their common history is a factor in their own continued cohesion. They pride themselves on being a group of kin and on being Welsh. Now only the women work together, and each successive failure of a social activity makes the next one more difficult to start. Improvements in public transport, television, radio and the cinema have already diminished the interest of the young people in the village and its affairs. Emigration in search of better economic and leisure opportunities is taking its toll. These developments decrease the number of cross-cutting ties which bind Pentre people into a community. As many of the older villagers fear, the time may come, if these developments continue, when the village ceases to be a village community and becomes merely a collection of dwellings, housing some of the industrial workers of Great Britain.

Clanship among the Tallensi: 'It is a cardinal principle of Tale social structure that every social grouping defined as a unit in one situation, or according to one principle, dissolves into an association of lesser and differentiated units in another situation or according to another principle.' Also Colson, E., 'Social Control and Vengeance in Plateau Tonga Society', *Africa*, 1953, has a similar statement.

BIBLIOGRAPHY

(a) WORKS CONCERNING WALES

Beacham, A., *Survey of Industries in Welsh County Towns* (1946-47), Oxford, 1951.

Borrow, George, *Wild Wales*, first published 1862.

Brennan, T., Cooney, E. W., and Pollins, N., *Social Change in Southwest Wales*, Watts, 1954.

Davies, Margaret, *Wales in Maps*, Cardiff, 1951.

Dodd, A. H., *The Industrial Revolution in North Wales*, Cardiff, 1951.

Evans, Hugh, *The Gorse Glen (Cwm Eithin)*, The Brython Press, Liverpool, 1948.

Evans, H. Meurig and Thomas, W. G., *Y Geiriadur Newydd (The New Welsh Dictionary)*, Llyfrau'r Dryw, Llandebie, 1953.

Griffith, Wyn, *The Welsh*, Penguin Books, 1950.

Harris, Kenneth, 'Wales', a series of articles in *Liverpool Daily Post*, from 3 August, 1953.

Jenkins, R. T., 'Development of Nationalism in Wales', *Sociological Review* XXVII, 1935.

Lloyd, Sir John, *History of Wales from the Earliest Times to the Edwardian Conquest*, London, 1911.

Mahler, M., *Chirk Castle and Chirkland*, London, 1912.

Rees, William, *An Historical Atlas of Wales*, Cardiff, 1951.

Thomas, Rev. D. R., *A History of the Diocese of St. Asaph*, London, 1874.

Tobit-Evans, H., *Rebecca and Her Daughters*, Cardiff, 1910.

Williams, C. R., 'The Welsh Religious Revival, 1904-05,' *British Journal of Sociology* 3, 1952.

Williams, David, *History of Modern Wales*, London, 1950.

GOVERNMENT REPORTS

Royal Commission on Land in Wales and Monmouthshire, 1893-96.

The Council for Wales and Monmouthshire: Second Memorandum, Cmd 8844, London, 1953.

The Place of Welsh and English in the Schools of Wales, H.M.S.O., 1953.

(*b*) GENERAL WORKS CITED

Arensberg, C. M., *The Irish Countryman*, New York, 1950; (and Kimball, S. T.) *Family and Community in Ireland*, Harvard, 1948.

Barnes, J. A., 'Class and Committees in a Norwegian Island Parish', *Human Relations* VII, 1954, I; (with Gluckman, M. and Mitchell, J. C.) 'The Village Headman in British Central Africa', *Africa* XIX, 1949.

Colson, E., 'Social Control and Vengeance in Plateau Tonga Society', *Africa* XXIII, 3, 1953; *The Makah Indians*, Manchester, 1953; 'Clans and the Joking-Relationship among the Plateau Tonga of Northern Rhodesia', *Kroeber Anthropological Society Papers* Nos. 8 and 9, California, 1953.

Curle, Adam, 'Kinship Structure in an English Village', *Man*, 100 and 242 (1952); 'What Happened to Three Villages', *The Listener*, 18 December, 1952.

Evans-Pritchard, E. E., *Witchcraft, Oracles and Magic among the Azande*, Oxford, 1937; *The Nuer*, Oxford, 1940; *The Sanusi of Cyrenaica*, Oxford, 1949; (with Fortes, M.) *African Political Systems*, Oxford, 1940; (and others) *The Institutions of Primitive Society*, Oxford, 1954.

Fortes, M., *Dynamics of Clanship among the Tallensi*, Oxford, 1945.

Gluckman, Max, 'Analysis of a Social Situation in Modern Zululand', *Bantu Studies* XIV, 1940, 1 and 2; *Rituals of Rebellion in South-East Africa*, The Frazer Lecture 1952, Manchester, 1954; 'Political Institutions', in *The Institutions of Primitive Society*, Oxford, 1954.

Homans, George, *The Human Group*, London, 1951.

Kempe, J., 'A Pilot Survey of Much Marcle', *The Sociological Review* XLI, 1949.

Kuper, L. and others, *Living in Towns*, London, 1953.

Loomis, Charles P. and Beegle, J. Allan, *Rural Social Systems*, New York, 1950.

Malinowski, B., *Crime and Custom in Savage Society*, London, 1926.

Mauss, Marcel, *The Gift: Forms and Function of Exchange in Primitive Societies*, London, 1953.

Mitchell, G. D., 'The Parish Council and the Rural Community', *Public Administration* XXIX.

Pitt-Rivers, J. A., *The People of the Sierra*, London, 1954.

Pomfret, J., *The Struggle for Land in Ireland, 1800-1923*, Princeton, 1930.

Roberts, Llewelyn, *Aids to Public Health*, 7th ed., London, 1952.

Schapera, I., *Migrant Labour and Tribal Life*, London, 1947.

Stewart, C., *The Village Surveyed*, London, 1948.

West, James, *Plainville U.S.A.*, New York, 1945.

Whiteley, Winifred, 'Littletown-in-Overspill' in Kuper, I., *Living in Towns*, London, 1953.

Whyte, W. F., *Human Relations in the Restaurant Industry*, New York, 1948.

Williams, W. M., 'Kinship Structure in an English Village', *Man*, 208 (1952).

Wilson, G. and M., *The Analysis of Social Change*, Cambridge, 1945.

INDEX

Activities, method of starting, 79, 87

Africa, parallel social behaviour in, 155, 155n, 156

Arensberg and Kimball, 54, 151n

Baptists, 17, 32, 47, 57; number of, 58; minister, 83 et seq.

Barnes, J. A., 14n, 73n, 156

Bench, 11, 69

Billiards, 52

Brass band, 19, 65-6

Brennan, T., 12n

British Legion, 31, 52, 54, 125

Bus services, 23, 33

Carnival, 53, 131-42; committee, formation of, 132 et seq.; finances of, 140, 143-4

Chapels, 12, 14; hostility to Church, 15-18, 58-63; and language, 32; and kinship, 47; and schools, 94; and football, 103

Church of England in Wales, 12, 14, 32, 43; fundamental difference from Chapels, 58-63; and outsiders, 61; and schools, 94

Class, economic, 11-12, 149; in local government, 67-8, 71, 85; in football committee, 109

Colson, E., 14n, 20, 155n, 156n

Committees, 18, 65, 66; of ratepayers, 73, 80, 83; importance of in recreation, 79; election procedure, 84-5; football, 103, 108-9; village control over, 107-8; resignations from, 108; secrecy in, 123; carnival, 132-3, 135-7; sup-

porters', formation and composition of, 146

Community, 40; cohesion of, 97-8, 100, 153-4

Conflict, devices to minimise, 18, 97, 98; exemplified, 130, 135 et seq.

Coronation, 13, 43, 53; and football, 120 et seq.

County Council, 11; class and, 67-8; public relations of, 78; and schools, 90, 91, 92

Courtship, 49, 51

Cousin marriage, 48-9

Cross-cutting ties, 157

Curle, A., 18n, 20n, 49n

Cycle of activities, 19, 130, 153-4

Devolution, Welsh, 75

Doctor, status of, 75

Dodd, A. H., 25-6

Donations to societies, 42-3

Drama groups, 16, 32

Dunnico, Sir Herbert, 63

Economy, village, 9-10, 23-7; effects of collapse of, 56

Education, 15, 81, 88 et seq.; see also under Schools

Eisteddfod, 63, 75, 124

Elfed, 63

Emigration, 51, 27

English influence, 24

English language, 11, 14, 30-1; and rural areas, 76

Evans, Huw, 45, 106n

Evans-Pritchard, E. E., 155n, 156n